MW00944227

101 Ways to Please a Woman

by

Lenaure Batista

AuthorHouse™
1663 Liberty Drive, Suite 200
Bloomington, IN 47403
www.authorhouse.com
Phone: 1-800-839-8640

First published by AuthorHouse 1/29/2009

ISBN: 978-1-4389-2686-5 (sc)

Printed in the United States of America
Bloomington, Indiana

This book is printed on acid-free paper.

To my Dad ~ who taught me so much,
with love and gratitude

CONTENTS

Acknowledgments

I am so grateful for the strong, beautiful women in my life ~ Ysabel, Rosa, Mary, Marcia, Denise, Cristina, Ralisa, Cely, Lina, Eva, Hazel, Lauri, Charlissa, Linda, Tor, Revelina, Oriolla, Cassie, Cheryl, Sandy, Betty, Rozania, Denise R., Trina, Joanne, Eleanor, Alice, Debbie, Shawana, Deborah, Nicole, and all the countless others that would take up this entire page. You ladies are amazing!

And to all the strong, wonderful men in my life ~ Marty, Corazon, Sean, Juan, Steven (BlackTide!), Giovanni, Chris, Michael, Roni, David C., Daryl, Pepper, Michael W., Deo, Ron D., Rick, myriad friends and colleagues. Thank you for all you are and all you do!

You have each touched my heart and enriched my life in a multitude of ways. I admire you, appreciate you and love you guys. To those of you that sat through my reading circle, thank you for your time, insight, laughter and realness. Can't wait for all the ones to come!

Emma, Max (and in memory of Cha Cha) – my beautiful, cutie pies… you keep me young and happy!

To all the happy couples out there, young and young at heart – keep up the great work! Your love is inspiring!

To the entire team at AuthorHouse ~ Thank you for your time, courtesy, talent and professionalism. I appreciate all of you!

To all those who have come before, who continue to guide me and show me the path -- Thank you.

Muah!

Lenaure

Introduction

Okay men of the world – this is it! We all know men are different from women, but the fact is men love women and women love men!! So I'm here to help you guys by offering you something that isn't easy to get -- the secrets of how to please your woman. Every day some man, somewhere says, "*There's just no pleasing a woman.*" Not true!! You just haven't been let in on the secrets and maybe you gave up too soon. Too often men, as a gender, seem to be on the outs with the fairer sex and they're always being told what they're doing wrong. Well I think that's pretty unfair, and it's got to be annoying to you. Now you're going to get to read about what women love, directly from the horses' mouths, so to speak. Real women's perspectives written to help out real men - finally!! Lots of men have some great ideas about some of the things that keep women happy. For the rest of you, this'll be a fun glimpse into stuff that we really like and that really turns us on.

Your woman is hot, gorgeous, sweet, intelligent, and into you – all great reasons for you to want to keep her happy and build a long, satisfying life with her. Let me point out, this is for men who want to grow with their partner and who want to get into the mystery of pleasing their woman, over and over, and over again. There should be NO MORE EXCUSES about not understanding what a woman wants. No more using the tired, old phrase "*It's impossible to please her*!" Or my favorite, "*Women, you can't live with 'em, and you can't kill 'em!*" Nothing is impossible – especially when it comes to pleasing us!

Here is your handy list with not 10, not 20, not 30, but 101 different things you should know and use to show that special lady in your life just how much she means to you. This guide is full of little secrets, so you better use them to make that woman glow with excitement! I'm trying to help bridge the gap that so many people are happy to point out but do nothing to fix. I think a man and a woman together is a beautiful thing, and I'm on the side of closeness, sexual and emotional fulfillment, romance, trust and togetherness. And ultimately, a more peaceful and fun coexistence between the sexes.

How did I get all this information from so many women? How do I know what women want? You might be asking these questions, so I'll tell you. I am a happy, healthy, educated woman who has had some really good relationships and also a couple of bad relationships with men. My life as a professional dancer, fitness trainer, consultant, performing artist, sister, cousin, friend, has put me in touch with literally thousands of people over the years, a majority of whom were women from all walks of life. I have heard enough complaints and stories and nightmares and fairytales to write twenty books! Our collective experience has been a great teacher. I realized long ago that so many women everywhere are saying and desiring the same things from the men in their lives. And so many men are saying so many of the same things about how they don't know what to do, how there's just no pleasing us, and how relationships don't do well after the first year or so. As an objective, third party listener, I've been hearing the same kinds of things coming in different ways from both sides. That inspired me to write something that will hopefully have a positive impact on relationships, instead of just another cynical and angry diatribe that will only encourage more male bashing and contribute to that widening gender gap. I have a lot of male friends and have met some great men over the years (and some not-so-great men too), so I wanted to do something to help the male population for a change because men and women pretty much want the same things, but we definitely have different ways of thinking and interpreting each other's words and actions.

There are books out there disguised as semi-positive tomes whose aim it is to give advice to women about how to 'snag a man,' or 'how to keep a man,' but they seem to be full of male-bashing concepts or outdated (damn near pre-historic) notions of proper female behavior, that really just incite anger in the readers. There are also books out there that bash women and relationships. Some of those books make it seem like the number one problem men have with women is that 'women are just too much work!' I'd just like to say that under no circumstances should mature adults assume that a successful relationship doesn't require work. That's just not realistic. Relationships do require work between the people involved. However, there shouldn't be a negative connotation on that idea of 'work.' Being in a great relationship might be compared to having the career of your dreams, or the house of your dreams, or the car of your dreams. All those things require a lot of work and maintenance, but when you love what you're doing or love living in a beautiful home, driving a gorgeous car or doing a job you're passionate about, it's not a grueling chore. It's work that you love and that fulfills you. If you think of your relationship as a dead-end job that you drag yourself to everyday just for the paycheck, or the hooptie-mobile that you drive from point A to point B, all the while praying that it doesn't strand you again, then of course you're not going to want to work at it. If you have such a bleak view of what a relationship is – some unfulfilling, monotonous chore that you perform with the bare minimum of exertion until you can finally move on, then of course you think of any relationship as too much work. You probably shouldn't be in one until you have a brighter outlook.

Essentially, many relationship books insist that one gender or the other is wrong and must change who they are in order to fit in with the other. That mentality is just wrong and a relationship based on that thinking will never work. We have to be who we are, on both sides, and learn how to finesse our way around our differences with respect and intelligence in order to have happy relationships. This book is for people who love what they have and where they are and are passionate about moving forward and growing. Those people will benefit most from this fun file of 'keep her happy' suggestions.

I asked tons of women to give me lists of their top 50 ways of being pleased by a man – that is 50 things they would love the man in their lives to do for them (or keep doing). Included among these women are many of my friends, colleagues and clients, that are beautiful and generally popular, healthy women of different ethnicities from various parts of the world. They are by and large, happy, independent and successful professionals in their late 20's, 30's and 40's, and a few in their 50's. I've had the pleasure of working with them and having friendships with them over several years. I also received lists from women I don't know, globally, through women's groups, sites, clubs, forums etc… generally of the ages 27-47. What truly shocked me was when I received so many of the same answers from all these people. That made it that much easier to put this list together than I initially anticipated. Women want to be and can be pleased, and pretty much want the same things from our men. Of course there are variations to our priorities, and naturally there are always exceptions to everything. But for the most part, women around the world have a great deal in common as far as desires go.

I also got feedback from men about what they think it takes to please women in general, or what has worked for the ones in happy relationships. All kinds of men sent me their views – married, single, happy, miserable, younger, older (average ages 29-52). What I definitely learned right away is that men think very differently from women and that they often arrive at a similar outcome by a totally different route. Many men give up on a relationship too early because they believe it's damned near impossible to please a woman and they don't want to work that hard. It's almost a given that if your starting mindset on this issue of pleasing women is one of it being an impossible goal, based on your past negative experiences or from hearing terrible things about the improbability of success, then you are almost doomed to fail because that's what you're expecting to do.

On the other hand, the happily married or engaged men in committed relationships share a very important mindset. Somehow they have figured out that if you make your woman happy you'll be a very happy and taken-care-of man. They also seem to understand that the opposite is also true. If your woman is unhappy or unfulfilled in the relationship, the whole dynamic and everyone involved will be impacted negatively. Happy men actually like the women they're with and enjoy being a couple. They understand that a relationship takes work, but it should be enjoyable work. So, wonderful men of the universe, this is your chance to do the right things with a smart guide that can help keep you in your woman's good graces – which is always a good thing for you.

Let me clarify my intentions a little further. I wrote this book for men who are already working on a relationship that they're interested in growing. It could also work for men who hope to meet that special woman someday soon and want to know what to do when the time comes. It's for good guys who are basically tired of winging it and want to get a clue, or who want a few dozen more clues. This is not a '*how to pick up chicks*' guide, nor a '*delusional fools guide for tricking a woman into staying with you who's not really feeling you like that*' book. I'm working under the belief that there are tons of good men out there who want to know what will not only make a woman happy, but what will keep her purring for years to come! Whether you're married with kids or single and getting to know each other, we all need to keep growing our love skills. This book will serve you well.

My only request when using this guide is that you actually care about the object of your desire and attention. This is not a player's guide to getting some booty. It wouldn't necessarily work for that and I would not want to be party to helping a player mess with some nice, sweet woman who's taking him seriously. Plus, that's just plain dumb! There's nothing worse than acting interested and enamoured merely to win the chase and get a notch on your score belt. It's pretty ruthless and pointless and can be devastating for everyone involved. If that's all you want, you can pick up some other book and just keep chilling solo at the club of your choice. It's much better to keep it real.

I hope this book of great, romantic suggestions and love-enhancing displays of affection and devotion will be used with good intentions. Let it be your guide to revealing your true interest for that special beauty in your life – while helping yourself become a more interesting, debonaire and thoughtful mate. If it is used in the right spirit, and you have chosen a worthy partner, your actions will surely be well-received and cherished. Your woman will reciprocate in turn and shower you with the simple, yet very important things that tell you she undoubtedly loves you right back! On the flip side, if you're really not feeling her on a 'long-term' basis or a 'this is love' and 'she's the one' kind of level, don't waste your time or her feelings – it only gets worse and more complicated with needlessly wasted energy. If this book is misused it will backfire and all hell can break loose! Don't call me when you have a pissed-off, scorned woman after you. You've been warned.

We all get those emails that make pretty funny comparisons between men and women. Like this little list translating how we think:

WOMEN'S ENGLISH	***MEN'S ENGLISH***
No = Yes	No = No
Yes = No	Yes = Yes
I am sorry = You'll be sorry	I am hungry = I am hungry
We need to talk = you're in trouble	I am sleepy = I am sleepy
Sure, go ahead = You better not	I am tired = I am tired
Do what you want = You will pay for this later	Nice dress = Nice cleavage!
I am not upset = Of course I am upset, moron!	I love you = Let's have sex now
Yeah, that was fun = Is that all you got?	Can I call you sometime? = Wanna have sex?

These lists poke fun at both sexes; women for not saying what we really want to say, and men for constantly having sex on the brain. I think we laugh because we agree with a lot of these stereotypical misunderstandings, but sometimes the differences in how we think and interpret things can lead to arguments and real trouble between us.

Yes, men and women can be very different, but if we take the time to learn what our partners really like and make use of some great suggestions, the gap between us will get narrower and the bonds of togetherness and trust that we want from each other can grow stronger.

With all that unity and reliance there will be little or no time left for misery, bickering, resentment and everything else that seems to plague clueless couples. It's just a lack of understanding, bad communication and lame effort that keeps the sexes at odds. That sounds easy enough to fix, but in today's world of instant gratification those three things inevitably end relationships time after time. Thankfully there are many couples that do have fulfilling lives together and hopefully this guide will help bring even more couples to that happy place where she feels special and is happy to take care of her wonderful man.

You can even do this for partially selfish reasons – you want her to be more into you and all over you – fine. Just remember guys, the right woman will reciprocate if she's happy, and the right woman will also walk away if she feels that you don't appreciate or understand what you have. We naturally and innately look to our men to take the lead in our relationships, to set the pace. – We WANT you to be the man! A happy woman will lovingly take care of her mate. Men are pretty easy to figure out, and I mean that in a good way. We know what you all want for the most part: sex, food, sports, sex, sleep, peace, toys, food, sex. Did I hit most of the points? Your woman has a very good idea of what you need, and here's your chance to figure her needs out. If you keep her happy, you will likely be one blessed, grinning fool – and I mean that in a good way too!! Learning some new tricks could be a win-win for both of you and will have a positive trickle effect on both your lives. I won't begin to tell you what having happy parents means to the lives of offspring for generations to come; we all have families, we've seen the good and the bad. But that's a topic for another book.

You basically lead by example – give and you shall receive, in every sense! The best leaders do it first, so take the lead in your relationship and you'll become a nice guy who finishes first! Trust me guys, a lot of this stuff is not going to be anything new or intimidating. Hopefully, you already know and do plenty of what's in here. But what this can do for you is act as your little secret weapon reference guide that you can use to keep your relationship spicy and fresh. Hey, you can also read it with your woman and then you'll get to know even more about her. Enjoy it. I wish you the best of luck and ask that you please send me your feedback.

I separated all the suggestions into categories to make it easy for you to see where they fit in their importance on the 'relationship points' scale.

The ones in this group mean they are a must – a basic point that every man should always do. These are fundamental requirements to build a strong foundation.

This group contains special and thoughtful gestures. They're important moves that show how much you really care. Woman adore a loving, thoughtful man, and will show their thanks with kisses.

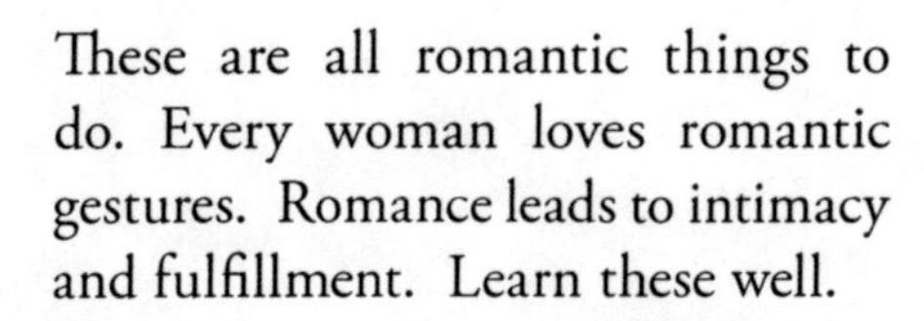

These are all romantic things to do. Every woman loves romantic gestures. Romance leads to intimacy and fulfillment. Learn these well.

This group is so sizzling hot that she might turn it all right back on you – in a good way. Be ready for fire and passion.

And finally, the ones in this group are considered part of 'the total package' – the right combination of skills and activities you can use to keep your woman smiling and keep your relationship hot like sunshine.

The order of these tips is not scientific, just a fun grouping of ideas based on the lists I received from so many people. At the end of the book you'll have the full list that you can refer to in emergencies. Also, don't get overwhelmed by all the suggestions. They're not meant for you to use them all or all at once. They're really just pointers to give you some good ideas to have fun with. Make them work for you. Cheers!

PART I: THE BASICS

START RIGHT, TAKE FLIGHT

1. Be honest and sincere with her and with yourself

This is KEY!!! You have to show who you are right at the beginning of your pursuit. Don't pretend to be some other guy who's suave, sophisticated, cultured, social, and nice if you're really a dorky, uneducated, angry, anti-social anarchist who hates people! You may fool your 'date' initially for a little while, but the true you will and does emerge. Why chase someone who isn't your match to begin with? Above all else, be honest about what you want from her - don't fool yourself and play a fool!

If you're real and upfront with what you're bringing to the table and what you like, on all levels, your honest presentation will put you in an environment you're naturally comfortable in, so you'll be much more likely to meet someone who's right for you. You're not faking it – it's all based on the real you. For example, don't go to a salsa club to meet a potential girlfriend just because there are pretty women there. Go because you like the music or want to learn how to dance, and then meet a pretty woman there. Then you'll have something in common when you meet that potential, special someone.

Just like decent men tend to be turned off by shallow, fake, plastic women, real women also hate shallow, phony, posing men. It's similar to people on the online dating services who post fake or old photos of themselves and then show up and wonder why the person they're meeting is not attracted to them. If you fake the funk to get the girl and then you reveal the true you and you're totally different from the initial 'you,' she'll feel cheated and resentful. That's never a good thing. Pretending, posturing and posing as something you're not will backfire on you sooner or later.

The same thing goes for much more serious issues like your status – hetero, bi-sexual, gay on the DL, HIV positive or negative, baby-daddy, divorced, separated, swinger, etc.... These are things your potential future wife or life-partner, or even 'just a girlfriend' has to know up front and go along with if she wants to be with you. This book is for guys thinking long-term with their woman. But even if you're not sure and you're just trying to see where the relationship can grow to, you have to start with honesty. Just imagine you have all these secrets you didn't reveal and then you end up really digging her, but now you have to backtrack and tell her all that stuff that should have come out at the beginning. She's going to feel like she's looking at a stranger because she doesn't know the real you at all.

If you have an STD, or you've had some risqué relationships, she needs to know before you become intimate, so she can decide for herself if she wants to go there. If you're bisexual or have some questions about your sexuality, you need to let your potential partner know ahead of time. Don't hide something so important just because you're afraid of rejection. This way you release that burden and won't have to keep lying. You should have enough courtesy to let her know the truth. If you're a swinger, then you need to end up with a swinger – don't spring it on your monogamous mate after being together for 5 or 10 months or years and expect not to destroy her faith and hurt her. You shouldn't make that decision for anyone no matter how tempting it might be or how worried you are about being rejected.

You may very well get rejected often – rejection is a part of life. Eventually you will meet someone who accepts you as you are. When you lie by omitting some crucial truths you are playing with fire and with someone's life, and you're probably not ready to be with anyone long-term. And, you're also hindering your own growth. Not worth it. Be honest with yourself and with her. Let your mate pick you based on the truth. The right match for you is someone you can be yourself with and who can be herself with you. She's someone you have similar interests with and not someone you have to impress with a bunch of made-up stuff. Imagine how close you can become with someone who knows the real you and wants to be with you because of it. Again, be honest; it's impressive and also necessary if you want this thing to take off in the right direction.

2. Be Free & Clear!

I can't tell you how many people I've known that have jumped into a new relationship before they were completely out of the previous one. This is not good and probably won't end well, so don't do it!

If you are in an unhappy marriage and thinking about ending it, or are already in the middle of a divorce, are living with someone and planning to move out, are seeing someone but haven't called it off yet, have broken up with someone recently, but still interact to help get her over you, or have any kind of major relationship baggage you're carrying around with you, listen to me carefully. YOU ARE NOT FREE AND CLEAR! Do not jump into something with someone else. You could potentially turn 'the one' into a rebound disaster just because you're not really available. You can't just be free in your mind or in your heart, or on paper – all your parts have to be on the same page. It's not fair to you and it's definitely not fair to the new woman, and this could make things with your ex or soon-to-be-ex get really ugly if she finds out. There are rare cases that I've heard of where two people got involved before they were completely over their previous relationships and the new romance lasted and even led to marriage, but I can count those cases on two fingers.

You need to be clearly done with your past relationship. You should have a completely fresh start so you can enjoy the beauty and excitement of a new romance. All your lessons learned should be neatly tucked in the appropriate folder of 'distant past' relationship lessons. You should not have issues pop up because of these unresolved problems and emotional demons you're still carrying around in your mind. You shouldn't still be suffering from financial nightmares caused by a previous mess and expect it not to mess with your current relationship. This happens when you don't get out of one thing before getting into another. You bring all your issues and drama with you and you will inevitably compare the present with the 'almost' past. That's never a good thing. I highly warn against this.

I'll talk about the importance of good timing later. But just for arguments sake, let's say you meet this wonderful person in the middle of getting out of something else. It may not be the best timing, but it happens and you feel like you've met someone really special, but you know you have to finish what's presently on your plate, so to speak. Let your desire to make the new relationship work be the rocket fuel that fires you up. Don't dawdle on something that's over and done just because it's a difficult or uncomfortable process. And don't use your 'new' relationship as the only reason to motivate yourself to change what's wrong with your life. You need to be a self-motivated man so that when you do meet someone worth your effort, you'll be ready for her. You can potentially blow something really great and lasting because you were too afraid to move on when you should have. Just like the new owner of a house would not put up with the previous owner remaining in residence there, your new woman does not want to deal with the residue of your old relationship in any way. That's a sure way to kill a romance before it even has a chance to blossom. Make sure you are free and clear. Remember, the basics are all about starting out with a strong foundation.

3. Be authentically nice and genuinely kind

This kind of goes along with being real, but it's all about you as a person in or out of a relationship. Don't pretend to be a nice guy when you're really an ass or a jerk to people outside of your relationship. When you're into someone, you should be inspired to be your best and to keep growing into a better version of yourself. But, you shouldn't wait to meet someone great before you start being that nice person. What you are is what you'll attract, so if you're not already doing this, start being the kind of person you'd like to be around. You'll become an even better you. Let that good feeling you get from being with your woman spread into the other areas of your life and enjoy it.

Where Does She Fit In Your Life?

4. Make her and your relationship a high priority in your life

Make sure you want to grow a relationship and have a future with this woman. Just like your education, your career, your hobbies, sports, etc..., you have to put time and energy into things you care about. Don't let your love interest be the last thing on your list. If you don't have time for a serious relationship, don't tell a woman you want to be exclusive. It's not fair to her to be waiting around for when you have little crumbs of spare time to throw at her. If you want someone in your life, then take the time to get to know her by spending quality time and having a lot of fun. Start to put her very high up on your list of importance. Talk to her about where you'd like to be in the next few years and include her if you'd like her to be there with you. Otherwise, just tell her you're not looking for anything serious and she'll know not to invest too much of her heart in you. Spirituality, financial freedom, your woman, etc…, she should be right up there with the big stuff until you both decide to become partners for life. You should intentionally take steps to grow that intimacy and closeness between you so she understands you're serious. A great relationship requires a lot of quality time to get to know each other. Creating time for someone is not always easy, but don't make any excuses. Just get it done.

5."She's Your Equal" doesn't mean she wants to be the man

This is so important for you to understand. More and more relationships fail to grow into happy marriages because many men feel intimidated by their woman's success. They feel that if the woman is a superstar at work she's somehow diminishing his masculinity in the relationship. Now I'm not saying this never happens, but often times is just a crock of crap. The men who might be experiencing this inkling need to change the way they interpret things. The more successful your woman is, the better it makes you look as her man. You should remember that she's a reflection of you in many ways, so you should be extremely proud of her success and happy to share it. Let's face it, woman have stepped up in education and in the business world, and we still don't get equal pay for equal work, so we have to work extremely hard to prove ourselves on the job. When a woman rises in any male-saturated field there should be a huge celebration at home. Also, just because she can pay for the same stuff that you can pay for, doesn't mean she doesn't want you to be the man. If you can share your success with her, then you should be happy to accept her success as well. If a woman feels the need to dumb herself down just to keep the peace at home, it won't be long before she'll have to choose between being happy and playing this self-defeating role.

By denying her true ability a woman creates a false sense of confidence for the man, and shoots her own self-esteem to hell. If she loses who she was when you first met her, just to make you feel better about yourself, eventually you won't recognize her and it'll be a lose-lose. If women accept the men in their lives the way they are, then men also need to accept their women. Every woman is not a Susie Homemaker or a kindergarten teacher, and that's a great thing. The mentality at work here seems to be that if a man is the superstar in the workplace, the woman will always admire him and look up to him and he is 'the man.' Whereas if the woman is successful at work then that somehow speaks poorly on the man as the provider. That's totally wrong. Your relationship shouldn't be about your jobs, so it's okay for her to be a huge career winner too. You should be equals, regardless of what your salaries are.

As long as you put great effort into making things work, there is no reason for you to feel inadequate just because she makes a ton of money. She is still a woman – soft, feminine, beautiful, sweet, tender and sensitive where you're concerned, and the more you can nurture that side of her that the rest of the world can't, the closer the two of you will grow. She wants you around for more than your finances. Part of what attracted you to her is also part of what makes her successful, so you should want her to keep growing. Don't get me wrong. Women don't have a problem with a man who makes more, is the main provider, etc..., but whatever the financial ratio between you is, she is still your equal, and also a woman. We can be both.

NO WHINERS, WHACKOS OR WINOS!

6. Be successful and stable

You have to be satisfied with who you are and where you're going in life in order to enjoy your life and your relationship today. If you're a miserable person, there's no way you'll have much to offer any other person. Make sure you are in a position to enjoy someone's company and are stable enough to make a positive difference in another stable person's life.

There is less pressure on men to be providers nowadays then there was back in our parents' generation. However, a woman realistically needs be with a man who can provide support for a family – should she choose to go there one day. No matter what you can argue about this, it's a reality of life that women carry babies in pregnancy and men don't, so their men have to be able to provide financial and emotional support to the woman and all potential children of their union. It's just the way it is. It doesn't mean you're going to actually have children, or that your mate wants to give up her career if she's got one. But, a quality woman wants a man who is carving out enough of a life that he's able to make room for that future family if and when it happens.

If you're in a relationship, you can best believe she's thinking about the future and what it would be like with you. Being successful and stable doesn't have to mean you're already wealthy and exactly where you want to be in life – success is a journey and an ongoing process.

However, a man should be independent and living relatively well with the means to at least carry a large portion of the fiscal responsibility of a future household, and he shouldn't have any dangerous addictions.

A woman doesn't want a man who is emotionally unstable, unable to care for himself, or who's always broke. Just like a man doesn't want that kind of woman. How can you possibly get to know each other if you can't do anything besides sit in front of a television? Also, having the woman always pay for dinners or vacations gets tiresome really quickly for her.

A woman wants a man to wear the pants in the relationship, so to speak. That includes being stable and happy, taking an active part in plans and decisions and sharing at least half of the financial responsibilities, if not more. Having a man who can potentially provide a good future for a family is very attractive to a woman who is serious about where she's going. That's the kind of woman most men want a future with. Financial success and emotional stability will give you that edge you need to keep a good woman.

Personal Hygiene Matters!

7. Be clean and neat

This is really important! Just like men like to see and have a gorgeous woman at their side, women want a clean and well-groomed guy. Make sure your nails and your ears are clean. And please take care of those teeth, lips and hands. Make sure you smell really good everywhere, and all the time. That includes your breath! Don't be a slob. It's a serious turn-off for us, just as it is for you. Take human bites when you eat and please hold your fork like a civilized man with your fingers, not with your whole fist like some cave man. Don't scratch your crotch or walk with a limp/swagger and please don't release any toxic gases unless you're in the bathroom!!

Also, take care of yourself physically. You don't need to have the body of Adonis, but you should be able to hold yourself up in bed and carry your woman if it becomes necessary. You want to keep feeling good about yourself and keep your woman feeling attracted to you. You know how easy it is to change her mood. The word "funk" should only be used when referring to good 70's music, not some deadly b.o. Cleanliness and neatness makes you more attractive and more edible. Your hygiene has to be on point. Trust!

LITTLE BOYS NEED NOT APPLY...

8. Be Independent

Just like a man doesn't want a gold-digging, needy woman who can't survive without his wallet or his hand holding her up, no woman wants a so-called man that she's got to 'do' everything for. Your woman is not a substitute for your mommy, so make sure you are over the bottle and nipple stage before you try to get serious with a grown woman. The only children she wants to raise are the ones that come out of her or that she officially adopts.

First of all, you've got to have your own place. You will not understand how to appreciate what you've got on any level, until you are solely responsible for yourself. If you're still living at home you're not ready for a serious partnership with anyone. You need to cut the cords, leave the nest and all that, and manage your own nest. It doesn't mean cutting your parents out of your life or diving into a situation that you can't afford. But it does mean learning to do for yourself first. Only then can you actually have something to offer another person. If this sounds so obvious I can't be serious, good for you! That means you're probably doing the right things for yourself already.

Women have to do for themselves – for the most part, they're no longer waiting until they're married to leave they're parents' house. An independent woman is very attractive to a man, so he'd better be independent himself. If you've never had to run an entire household – cleaning, shopping, preparing meals, budgeting, paying all the bills, etc…, then you just don't know what it's like to be independent. If you're over 28, living on your own is a must. Not only will you have a place for you and your woman to spend time together, but you'll be in a position to move to the next level as a couple.

An independent man is sexy. A woman doesn't mind doing stuff for a man who doesn't demand it or expect it. A needy man who can't take care of his own basic needs definitely won't be able to keep up with an independent woman. I briefly dated a cute guy who had decent values, and was funny at times, but who turned out to be both financially and emotionally needy. How long do you think that lasted? Uh, yeah. Financial and emotional independence is required and it's also hot!

Set a Good Pace

9. Start small and slow and grow from there

This means don't shower her with everything you've got, pulling out all the stops right at the beginning just to catch her and then fizzle out once 'you're in.' Aside from the first three basic must-do's, this is probably the most important piece of advice I can offer any smart man for growing a long-term relationship. The key word is 'grow.' You have to crawl before you walk, before you run, etc..., so take the time to grow your relationship. Pace yourself. Get to know each other. Don't rush it along at some frantic pace. True romance with your match is a long-term and hopefully life-long process, like a neverending dance.

We all know unhappy couples or co-workers who talk about how terrible their marriage is, how they 'never get any' after the first year of being together, or how 'she used to want it all the time in the beginning' when they first started dating. That usually has more to do with them losing momentum and killing the romantic sparks than with her losing her libido. Trust me, if it's good, and you have a connection outside of the bedroom, most women want it All The Time!

Instead of giving her flowers and dinner and jewelry and trips and gifts, etc..., all in the first weeks and months, unless you can keep that adrenalin rush up forever, think longer term. Plan actual dates and activities that don't necessarily break the bank, and fill the time in between your dates with small, thoughtful gestures. Flowers at work once in a while, a nice love note for no special reason, and time where you're just getting to know each other, are a good start. Lots of phone calls, movies, intimate dinners, playing sports and long walks are great 'pacers' to keep you going in between the big romantic moves. Save the bigger gestures like jewelry and trips for really special occasions – her birthday, a special holiday, a 6-months-together dinner, a romantic weekend getaway, etc....

Pace yourself and you'll also remain excited. You don't need to have a relationship based on gifts, but they are really nice and fun to receive and give, so make sure you keep them coming. Don't get complacent and give up the chase just because you're comfortable with her. Time things right and let the quality of the moves you make escalate slowly as your feelings grow. This is your mate, your match, possibly your future wife if you choose to go down that path. So you have to keep that fire burning for the long run. If you're already in a long-term relationship and you'd like to rekindle some of those embers that died out, you'd better read fast and start catching up!

10. Never Give up the Hunt – Chase her, pursue her, woo her

All the happy couples I heard from or know have this in common. The man courts the woman and keeps pursuing her throughout their relationship. She, being very satisfied and secure, keeps taking good care of him. They keep dating and falling in love with each other. I'm not suggesting you become an obsessed lunatic stalker who doesn't let the girl breathe or have any space. Let me reiterate this is a guide for normal, healthy guys who have a special woman in their life that they want to please. When your woman is happy, you'll be very happy, and you'd better believe the reverse is true. An unhappy woman can make life pretty unhappy for the man neglecting her, because she won't be inspired to be all in it or in it at all. Find new ways to have fun adventures together.

She's the pulse of the relationship. Remember you're setting the pace and the energy. You're the fuel – like that song says, "Dame mas gasolina." Sounds cliché, but a woman needs fuel to keep her engine going. Although I'm not sure that's what the song was implying, she needs you to keep things fueled by continuing to pursue her. Courtship is an endless dance – you choose the steps and the level of excitement. Men were born to hunt. You just have to keep pursuing the same woman. You have to chase her if you want to keep her in your life. Many older men realize the fun of romance in their golden years after the love of their life has passed away and they're forced to find a reason to go on living. They often regret not doing more while they had a chance. Wouldn't it be great to understand much earlier in life that chasing your woman throughout your relationship will keep you both youthful and healthy and very much in love for a whole lot longer? Well now you know - get to it!

You Gotta Let Her Know!

11. Express Yourself

The only reason people should get together is to improve each other's lives with their presence and sharing moments of fun and pleasure. If you are going to be in it, then give it your all and express how happy you are about it. It will make everything that much more exciting for both of you.

A man can make a woman glow and blush and look absolutely radiant by expressing to her how important she is to him or how happy she makes him. An intimate partnership between two loving adults is one of the most amazing and powerful connections we can make, so of course it's crucial to express the good stuff you feel. The more you express, the sooner you'll find out if you have a lot in common. You can't discover much if you don't talk about stuff that you're feeling.

Some people are hooked on only expressing their anger or distaste, and they take everything else for granted. They spend their time criticizing and complaining and as a result, lose that spark in the bedroom too. This is a huge mistake in a relationship which can kill a budding romance. Being expressive has to be the rule in your relationship – even more so, because this is someone who is sharing herself with you and presumably you like being with her. You absolutely have to rise to the occasion and let her know that you are happy to be in it with her on a regular basis.

Too many guys hold back their feelings because they think it will make them appear 'whipped' or weak and cause her to walk all over him if he's too nice, or he'll lose one of his gonads for admitting he's into her. That's a self-defeating thought process. Sometimes it's just a lack of practice at being expressive that makes men continue to hold everything in. There are relationships that are worth stepping it up for. You've got to recognize when you're in something worthwhile and just go for it. Expressing your happiness to your mate doesn't make you some sort of soft pansy – it will actually make you appear stronger and more masculine because it will solidify your relationship and make her more secure in knowing where she stands with you. Whatever you believe and say is what usually comes to pass. The ripple effect of expressing what she means to you is she'll be more comfortable being open with you and you'll get even closer, have a stronger union and have an even better thing going.

Another reason guys clam up is because they're not sure if she's the one and they don't want to trap themselves in a relationship they're not certain about. Every relationship is a chance you both take on each other. If you never get close because you are too afraid to show the girl how you really feel, you could be missing out on the best thing that walked into your life. I've heard of this happening a lot with some of my male friends and their friends too. Inevitably the guys end up messing up that one relationship they should have held on to. Both the woman and the man end up moving on – the woman usually because she can't wait anymore for that expression of love that just isn't coming, and the guy because the woman is no longer giving him her time and energy. It's a lose-lose and could be avoided if you just take that chance.

The truth is you just won't know unless you give it your all. Yes, there is a possibility that things may go wrong and you could get your feelings hurt, but if you pick a mate based on honesty and who's into you and has things in common with you, the chances are if you dive in, she will too and you'll find a treasure. Women love expressive men. They make us feel like they're strong and in control. A man who knows how to express himself is really hot and it's a serious turn on for his woman. Practice this.

FLATTERY WILL GET YOU EVERYWHERE!

12. Compliment her

Ever heard the expression, "You catch more bees with honey?" Language is very powerful. You can make or break a deal, change a career, and affect someone's life, depending on what comes out of your mouth. When dealing with difficult people you'll get much farther with kindness than you will with combativeness or abrasiveness. Just imagine how much good you'll do in your relationship with the woman you love. Human beings thrive on positive reinforcement from others. We love to hear nice things from the people we care about. Too often people only speak when something displeases them, and they don't take enough time to vocalize positive things – they just assume the person in question knows how they feel.

In a world where women have it so extremely difficult, having to be beautiful, smart, thin, fit, shapely, gorgeous, independent, motherly, sexy, smart, sweet, tough, soft, strong, feminine, hot, conservative, etc... - you know how long that list is! We get all sorts of mixed messages, to say the least. So you should be the first one who tells her she's wonderful in the morning and the last one to tell her she's beautiful at night. It doesn't matter what she looks like. Don't compare her to anyone you've seen airbrushed in a magazine or well-lit on film. Don't compare her to other women you encounter. You don't like to be compared to other men, and she doesn't like comparisons either. She's uniquely wonderful and your reality is that this beautiful, interesting woman is in your life, and you're blessed to have each other. She's with you and you need to fill her head with encouraging, nice things about herself, so she'll keep being that beautiful, happy, grounded woman who loves to be around you.

A lot of men mistakenly think that women who like to hear compliments are weak or insecure. That's a pretty lame defense for not complimenting her – hang it up. We all enjoy being complimented and hearing nice things about ourselves, especially from our loved ones.

It's not just women – guys like to hear how handsome they are and how proud we are of them. They like to hear how strong and masculine they are and what wonderful upstanding pillars of society they are. Men compete for trophies on every level in life, every single day. There's nothing weak or insecure about enjoying sincere admiration. So again, lead by example.

No, she doesn't need to hear you say nice things, but she will enjoy it, so why not make her happy? You better believe some other guy somewhere throws compliments at her every chance he gets, just in case she's listening. It's good for you to keep yourself in the mix. Say nice things about her often. She'll remember you saying it and that will help keep her focus where you want it to be. Start right now; call her and tell her she's beautiful.

STAND OUT IN A CROWD!

13. Be respectful and respectable

People like to be around a stand-up guy. There's this positive energy that upstanding men exude. These are really good guys who do the right thing, treat people well and are generally well-liked. Aside from it being the right thing to do, a man who truly treats his woman with respect will in turn earn more of her respect and affection. It's about treating her like she's someone important in your life, whose opinion counts, whose feelings matter, and who is your equal. Don't just pay lip service to that notion, but actually believe it and act on it. Walk next to her, not in front of her. Don't leave her at the table eating just because you're done. Accept her opinion and her way of doing things as valid even if it's different from what you're used to. Just because you don't do things the same way, doesn't mean her way is wrong, and vice versa.

Too often men bully their women into changing their minds about any little thing. Or, they demean them into questioning their own opinions. Some men try to morph women into these little robots that behave and dress in a manner that pleases the man, with little regard for what she's already accomplished without him. Talk to her, not at her. This is a major issue with women who talk about their exes. The key word here is ex. Some guys are used to being brutish and a little abrasive with their friends and other male peers. When they get comfortable with their wife or girlfriend, they let some of that brutish bullying sneak into their relationship. A woman is not like your male mates. Don't treat her like one of your macho buddies to that extent. It's never good to use bullying or 'friendly' insults with your woman. You won't win in any way, so don't go there.

You also have to be a respectable person – someone who sees value in others. You have to be well-grounded and able to get along with people in general, meaning you are courteous and decent to other people. Some people are rude and disrespectful and act in a socially non-congenial manner. Basically, they're jerks.

How you feel about other people and how you treat other people in general reflects how you feel about yourself and will affect how you treat your mate. You can't expect to have a nice, sweet woman be all into you if you're generally not respectful of others. Are you someone who criticizes others constantly and cracks jokes on people and on your mate? Is it really funny or is it mean-spirited and demeaning? If your mate or some poor stranger is the butt of your jokes, that's disrespectful and hurtful, and it will cost you. Don't be a bully and don't pick on her or anyone else.

Why not figure out how to push her happy buttons and be a general mood lifter? That's what this guide is for. Not only will you refocus your energy into a positive activity which will help you as an individual, but you will treat your woman in a way that pleases her, is respectful and uplifting. A benefit to you both.

15. Be a perfect gentleman

A woman loves a man who knows how to treat her like a lady. He opens doors for her, walks behind her on the way out of a restaurant with his hand placed gently on the small of her back. He reaches across a table to hold her hand. He asks her if she would like to take a cab rather than walk, etc.... A gentleman takes care of his woman's physical welfare and looks after her comfort when they go out. And never makes a scene or embarrasses her in public. When she's with you, she wants to be treated like a dainty, classy beauty that you're proud to be with.

Don't mistake a gentleman for a doormat. You should not be anyone's lapdog who just obeys commands, carries bags and takes orders. A gentleman thinks for himself, but he's got her in mind. He knows her desires and acts in a refined manner without being asked to do so.

WHO SHE IS, IS WHO YOU GET!

16. Know her, Accept her, Love her.

Many people go into a relationship all excited at first and then proceed to try and change their partners. Women and men are both very guilty of this. I think people need to take more time getting to know each other as friends before getting emotionally attached. You should agree on all the big issues – the big seven as I like to call them – 1. Finances, 2. Commitment/Loyalty, 3. Sexuality/Monogamy, 4. Where to Live/Climate, 5. Raising a Family or not, 6. Religion/Spirituality, and 7.Drugs/Smoking/Alcohol.

There are habits like smoking, drug use, spending and saving style, religious beliefs, etc..., that are deal breakers for most people, so certain people should never get together even if they are initially attracted to each other physically.

If you can agree on the big stuff, you should be able to work through the small differences. But ultimately you have to accept the person you choose just the way they are right now, not some potential future version of that person. You can't be with someone hoping to morph her into something better and different than she is right now. If you accept each other as you are, you will have a better chance of staying together and being happy as you grow and change through life.

And let me lay it out for you overly critical guys. Women are not going to look like magazine covers most of the time. The people on the covers don't even look like that themselves. We're talking about hair extensions and wigs, tons of makeup that would be scary in person, professional lighting and a stylist and set director that makes sure that each cover shot is perfect. Then you have the magic of airbrushing and Photoshop editing to blur the fine details of cellulite dimples, small or saggy breasts and all the other imperfections that are human.

If your woman is attractive in person, you better believe she's probably better looking than many of the people you see on those magazine covers. I'm not bashing cover girls or celebrities, because they're just doing their jobs and the magazines are just trying to get more sales, but I'm trying to give you a realistic perspective.

How many times do you see a really pretty woman walking with a mediocre at best, sometimes balding, sometimes chunky and average guy? It's actually pretty common. Women work hard to look good, but they're willing to accept a man for his personality and other factors even if he's not as physically attractive as she is. Now let me ask you this? How many times do you see the reverse of that? A gorgeous, six foot tall, dark and handsome, straight man walking with a frumpy, balding, overweight, average-on-a-great-day woman? Probably never!!

The truth is women are more accepting of physical flaws in men because they fall for the whole package, not just the outward appearance. Men should return the favor. Don't get caught up in that shallow trap. Appreciate her the way she is. If you grow and change, great. But acceptance and love are the key. Hopefully you'll be there with each other to support and celebrate each step forward in your lives. A woman wants a man who's on her side and helps to keep her feeling good about herself by accepting her the way she is and accepting her decisions for her life. It's very similar to the kind of loyalty a man wants.

I think this is something that men and women have in common. We all want to be loved and accepted. Women want a man who can see the real us – not the big, bad woman that takes on the world each day. We want a man who loves the girl who wakes up with no makeup on and with tousled hair, but who also appreciates the woman in pinstripes and pumps and perfect makeup (or whatever her daily uniform is) who leaves the house to face the world. You've got to be her biggest fan and her life coach, and she has to be yours too. You've got to have her back because she's giving you her time, love and affection.

Are You On The Team, or Just Wearing The Colors?

17. Be committed to her

Wishy washy is terrible. Wishy washy sucks. You've got to be in it solidly and act with intent consistently, not just sometimes. Don't blow in the wind like a plastic bag. That's not to say you've got to be psychotic and totally head over heels from day one. But, you also can't say you're in an exclusive relationship and then always be the one on the hunt, looking for someone to upgrade her with. Even if you don't act on it and you're just looking to see if you still have your mack and your mojo with other women. It's going to hurt your relationship.

You wouldn't want the woman you're into to be fickle and flirt with every guy she encountered or even worse, date them. How could you ever trust her then? So, don't be that guy either. It's better to just date casually until you meet someone you want to give more of yourself to.

Be the guy that knows what he wants and knows she's standing right in front of him. Be committed even when she's not around. Be proud that you've got this great person in your life. If you can't tell the world about your relationship with a happy smile on your face, then why be in one at all?

If you're on a team you should be proud to wear the colors. If you couldn't care less who's jersey you wear, then you need to go back to the junior league.

Take charge of your relationship's future just like you plan your career and where you live. Talk to her and tell her where you'd like to go with your relationship. Show her that you're passionate about being with someone that you're so compatible with and that you'd like to grow with. That's so sexy.

If either of you have acquaintances or friends that create problems or lead you into precarious situations like strip clubs or pick-up bars, then obviously those are not people you can continue to hang with at the same level once you're in a relationship with someone you care about. Once you're exclusive, she shouldn't be hanging out with her single, male friends (who you know like her like that), and you shouldn't be hanging out with your single, female friends either. If you're serious about someone there are certain behaviors you have to let go of. You can keep those relationships at a distance, but only if they respect your relationship with your mate. If there are other women around, then your woman should be invited also. And likewise, if there are other guys around for her outing, then you need to be invited as well. That way everyone knows where you both stand and that's what's up.

When you're truly committed, you cut that bachelor and bachelorette mentality out and you plan your life and your future together. That requires not dating other people and not sleeping around or even wanting to. And yes, at some point in the near future it means a ring and a serious question to be asked that will get you to the next level. If you're already married, put some fresh zest into your home life. Celebrate each anniversary with big gestures. Whatever your current status is, be totally in it and make the most of it. Be all in it and you're likely to win.

Lend Her Your Ears!

18. Listen

This is another basic that often falls to the wayside. Good communication is another major area that happy and successful couples have in common. Old married couples (20+ years of marriage) and young married couples all say communication is a must. A lack of communication breaks your relationship down and creates opportunities for dumb arguments that can lead to hurtful words and breakups. Successful people are good listeners in general and end up acting and adjusting their direction based on what they have heard. The same skill can be used in your relationship.

A smart man will listen to what his woman is saying and act on it. Some women (and men) stop communicating if they feel like they're not being heard, or if everything they say is turned against them. So when your woman tells you something like, "I need to know where our relationship is going," or "I want us to spend more time together," you really need to hear it and listen. If a woman has to say this at all, it means you're either not making any effort to move forward with her in your life, or you're not giving her the kind of time she would like. Don't just change the subject and pretend you didn't hear her. If you don't hear her and you miss something important like, "I don't like this," or "I love this," it will inevitably lead to her saying, "You never listen to anything I say."

If you listen to her and take an interest in what she feels and where she wants to go in life, then you'll likely be able to work on whatever issues come up. This goes along with being a good friend and is a basic requirement. Romantic relationships and friendships are two-sided gifts we have the chance to nurture and develop. Listening to each other is crucial for the success and longevity of your relationship.

Positively Sexy!

19. Be positive

Being positive is sexy. This might seem obvious, but surprisingly it was on enough lists that I had to include it on my basics list. Nobody likes a pessimistic humbug. They usually don't really like themselves and people generally avoid getting close to them. The worst feeling is coming home or picking up the phone to share an idea, or some plans or a decision with your partner and having him shoot you down cold with his negativity and cynicism. It's bad enough that there are so many dream killers out there waiting to bring you down. When that dream killer happens to be your own partner, it'll either chase you away (if you're resilient and lucky) or break you down and swallow you up.

Negativity totally deflates you and takes the joy out of your life for the moment. It makes you add another brick to that wall that can ultimately separate you from others for good. On the other hand, people gravitate towards positive people like bees to honey. A former co-worker of mine used to see the constant motion and excitement around my desk at work and would say all the time, "That girl is like a honey pot – the bees just can't stop buzzing!" I thought that was the funniest analogy. People were constantly stopping by my desk for information and feedback on work-related issues, when they could have saved themselves a trip and sent me an email or picked up the phone instead. I like to think I was stirring things up at work because of my positive vibe. Good energy causes a commotion in and of itself.

Just like positive energy spreads and attracts more positive energy, the same is true for negative energy. You can choose to spread either good or bad, it's totally up to you. Why not focus on spreading and growing that positive pulse with your example and your own good energy? You'll get more of what you want and you'll be contributing to the greater good.

Life can be tough and it's not always easy to stay positive, but it's up to us to make the most of whatever we are handed. Try this experiment. Purposely become a positive force. Start to notice what is changing in your life. See what kinds of people start becoming attracted to you. Find things to be grateful for every single day. You'll see how certain aspects of your life start to change for the better. Be positive and stay positive for you and your mate's sake. Brightness and positivity is magnetic and sexy.

Act Like A True Dog!

20. *Be loyal*

Oh boy. Down boy! I'm using the dog analogy in a truer sense than it's normally used. Dogs are completely loyal to their owners and their love has no boundaries or conditions. I'm not suggesting that humans are capable of this. I'm merely suggesting that we all give it a shot. The kind of loyalty I'm speaking of is far deeper than keeping your penis in your pants when you're away from her. You have to keep your tongue in your mouth, your eyeballs in your head, your neck from swiveling at every female that goes by, and your thoughts as loyal as possible. Yes, there are attractive people everywhere. Yes, men's behavior is often excused as some kind of primal urge to mate all the time. Blah, blah, blah! Guess what? Women have those urges too – hence the whole mating thing! If you're really into your woman and you want things to last, you have to be truly loyal. You shouldn't be secretly lusting after every other woman while forcing yourself to stay physically loyal out of obligation. Loyalty also includes not destroying your brain cells with gobs of internet porn, or sexual, internet interaction, which has been called another form of cheating.

True loyalty is when you stay with someone because you really want to be with that person. Again, honesty comes into play. People don't put up with crap like they used to "for the sake of the family," but there is still tons of lying and cheating going on out there, on all sides. It's seriously destroying the male-female relationship. Yes, there are cartloads of temptations via tight clothing, music videos, desperate people throwing it freely at unavailable men and women, and pornography everywhere. But is that an excuse to betray the person you truly want to be with? No. It's like throwing your mate and your relationship under the bus at every turn just because she's not there to witness your bad behavior. That's not healthy. So grow up and keep it in your pants (literally and figuratively) or else you both lose.

On the other hand, a couple that knows they're both loyal and can trust each other even in this sea of disease-spreading cheaters and liars and baby-daddies and baby-mommas, are going to have a chance at a great life together. They actually have a chance at making it in the long run. They likely have hot, hot vibes between them. Loyalty makes women happy. True loyalty makes you and your woman want each other more, and that's a really good thing.

Focus, Focus!!

21. Give her your undivided attention

This one goes along with being committed, but again it focuses on her and it's seriously important. Let me just say, this was on every single list I received from all the women who responded to my request, so it's really important! Women live in a cruel world where physical perfection is required at all times in order for us to have value, or so we're told through so many different mediums. Women are out here killing themselves to pay for fake boobs, fake hair, fake eyes, fake teeth, nails, butts, etc... If only you knew!! Women spend tens of thousands of dollars and so many hours on cosmetic improvements, enhancements, adjustments, augmentations, diets, gym memberships and liposuctions, lasers and waxings. You name it! We've either done it, know someone who's done it, thought about it, researched it or planned it for ourselves or our friends. Guys are feeling the pressure to look good and stay young too now, but it's still unfairly a woman's burden. Men are told they get refined with age. Women supposedly just get old and ugly. That's messed up.

The media tells us every single moment that we're not pretty enough, good enough, smart enough, hot enough, tall enough, small enough, thin enough, or some other 'not' attractive enough to catch some elusive perfect man whose approval and acknowledgment we live for. We know it's all b.s. crap, but the fact is, our whole society runs on that superficial and shallow mentality. If you don't look like the 'it' girl whose publicist paid big bucks to get her on the cover of 'The 100 Most Beautiful People' issue, then you supposedly just don't cut it in our society. There's constant pressure to look sexier, be hotter and more successful, but at the same time remain conservative enough to be taken seriously. What kind of crazy, confused message is that?! The least a man can do for his woman is show her that all her hard work pays off by giving her his full attention.

We live in a world filled with beauty, so you shouldn't be acting like a teenage boy at a girl's slumber party every time you're out and about with other attractive people around. Maturity and decorum are required when you're in an adult relationship. Aside from being generally aware of your surroundings, you should focus on who you're with.

A gorgeous, model friend of mine was dating a guy who seemed great. He was nice-looking, smart, financially stable, funny and athletic. They seemed to have a lot in common and she was hoping to get closer to him. They would get a lot of attention wherever they went. She was fine with that because it was the norm for her, but he let it go to his head. Before long (they had only been dating about 3 months) she started telling me that they couldn't be anywhere in public without him turning into a bobble-headed, woman-ogler, paying attention to everyone around him and ignoring her. He would make eye contact and flirt with any woman who would walk by. My other friends and I (male and female) even noticed it on a few occassions when we were all out as a group, and we could see that our girl friend was really embarrassed. She even asked her boyfriend a few times if he had someplace else he'd rather be to see if he would get the hint. No matter who you're with, if you are out with any person, you shouldn't have the attention span of a gnat. This is especially true if you're with your girlfriend and you want to keep her.

My friend would call me and tell me she felt like she was dating a stranger who was obsessed with 'walking the red carpet' everyday. He showed her one side of himself that she fell for and as soon as he felt he was 'in' he showed his true self. I think he broke every 'basic' rule that I've already listed in this book so far. Instead of keeping his woman happy, he figured he was the man and could have his cake and eat it too. My friend is a really confident and beautiful girl, but she started to feel badly about her relationship and also doubt herself. She had enough self-esteem to know that rude is rude and she wasn't having it, so that was that. She said she tried to hang in there with him for almost 2 years, patiently waiting for him to get the 'attention-starved' behavior out of his system, and she was waiting for the super nice guy she had known him to be for the first few months to come back. She finally dropped him and moved on. Why should she waste more time feeling bad over someone who wasn't into her enough to respect her and grow up? He admitted later that he had never had that much attention from women and he got caught up in the excitement of it all.

Here's a tip guys: many men fail to understand that there are insecure women out there who do this dumb, catty thing to attractive women who have a man at their side. They do their best to distract her man's attention, even for a second, just to have 'one up' on that pretty woman that they don't even know. It's so petty and ridiculously immature, but it goes on all the time, especially with young women. Don't get fooled into thinking it's about you. Even if you're a great looking guy, these women could care less about you in particular – and I mean no offense by that. The women being flirty only want to distract you from the person you're with for as long as possible. This happens so often and it can be a serious detriment to couples unless the guy is mature enough to see what's going on. Like what happened with my friend's ex. Women who do this to other women have really low self-esteem or they're desperate for some attention, or they're just not nice people. They want what your woman has even if it's just for a second or two. By getting your attention in a sense, they're getting you to disrespect your own woman, and apparently that makes their day. Guys are susceptible to this cheap form of attention. But all it does is make your woman pissed off and now she's looking at you differently, like you don't get it.

Please note, the woman you're with will always notice what you're doing even if she says nothing, and she's gauging your seriousness and maturity by how you handle different situations. This includes constantly taking calls on your cell phone, making eye contact or flirting with other women, and just not being focused in general.

Happy men in strong relationships understand this unwritten rule about focus. Your relationship should be about the two of you, not the two of you and a bunch of other people. Remember, if you let go of a good woman, there are usually no do-overs. When she's done with you,

you're out, off the team, finito, bye, bye! On the other hand, the respect you show her works in your favor. Your woman is doing the same thing for you because guys out there are just as nasty and would love to get her away from you, especially if she's really hot. It's so grade-school, but it's out there and it can mess up your evening and your close bond if you let it. Don't be so flattered by a stranger's attention – it's insignificant compared to the attention of the woman next to you who actually knows you and cares about you.

The bottom line with this is you have to be focused on the person you're with if you want her to focus on you. For some people it's a no-brainer. They don't have this issue. But for lots of people, it's a serious dilemna. Many guys try to say things like, "Hey, I'm a guy, that's what guys do." Or they'll say, "I know, I hate my cell phone, but what if I miss an important call?" Again, don't make excuses. Just treat her the way you'd like her to treat you.

You get to show your loyalty and interest in her every time you're out. So focus. Your woman will appreciate how special you make her feel and she'll reciprocate. I wanted to really drive this point home because once we decide to grow up and have something strong that lasts, there are behaviors we need to let go of and things we need to work on and be aware of. Focusing on each other and tuning out the world will do wonders for the relationship. For one thing, it will probably lead to more talking, laughing, kissing, and more intimacy. Trust – your woman expects and loves to have your undivided attention.

Keep It Simple, Some of the Time...

22. Date Night: Dinner and a Movie

Okay, this counts as two (just kidding). It's important to establish some traditions in your relationship right from the beginning, so I'm keeping this suggestion as one of the basics. There are times when we just want to watch a good movie and eat a good meal. If your mate is your movie partner, that's one more thing you can do together, one more thing you have in common. And, of course you always have to eat, so you might as well turn it into a dinner and a movie date. Make a night of it – find a new bistro or hit your favorite one and enjoy yourselves. Traditions create bonds that keep relationships growing in the right direction. Even simple ones like a weekly or bi-weekly dinner and a movie can provide that romantic setting that leads to greater intimacy. Taking turns picking your next dinner or movie gives you something to look forward to and keeps you interactive in a simple and fun way.

START SHOWING HER YOUR HEART

23. Open up to her

This is probably the hardest thing a man will ever do with anyone. Sharing the real you is a scary thing, especially for guys who are expected to be the pursuers, the providers, the strong ones. No one wants to be rejected, and even though a guy is in a stable relationship with someone who truly cares about him, in the back of his mind he still has that fear of being judged and getting rejected for some part of who he is.

The only way to build intimacy is to take steps to get closer to her by trusting her to share your life and get to love the real you. Again, you need to treat each other like friends first. You don't just pour your whole life story out in one afternoon and scare each other half to death. But rather share the big, important things early on in your relationship, and share tidbits of your childhood and your likes and dislikes slowly during your time together. It's got to be mutual sharing. You both have to listen and talk in order to create that balanced, reciprocal understanding, respect and closeness that comes from sharing your story and taking a chance on someone who's special to you.

When you share your feelings. Women often leave you. Maybe its younger women who mess it up for older women.
Men get there hearts broke

PART II – THOUGHTFUL & SWEET

24. Have FUN!!

This is just par for the course, but it's something people don't always do. Aside from eating out and seeing the latest films, you should include other fun activities in your monthly schedule. After all, this is the reason you want to be in a relationship in the first place – to have fun with someone, including, but not limited to just sex. We're all busy working and running around taking care of business and family, so we really need to enjoy our time away from the obligatory nine to five. Most people can't spend the entire week partying, so the one or two days they have completely free should be as fun-filled as possible. That's the whole point of being with someone – FUN!

You don't have to wait until you can afford a treasure hunt in Madagascar or skiing in Vail to have fun dates. You can just try to get two or three new things in every month. Try a salsa class or go see a new exhibit at the museum. Go see a live jazz or blues set or go to a dance concert. If you're both into sports, hit the batting cages or go indoor rock climbing. Go bikeriding at the park, take up cooking, sign up for a co-ed boot camp.

Whatever it is, make sure you consider both your tastes when planning it. If you're outdoorsy, but she's got allergies, don't plan a weekend of camping in the Spring – she'll be totally miserable, and so will you as a result. Part of being a happy couple means that you think of the other person; you consider someone beside yourself. You should love being with each other, and if you do, then you'll have even better memories when the two of you do fun activities together. Doing enjoyable things as a couple can be challenging and exciting. It's a great way to grow closer to your love interest and keep that spark alive. Physical activity also creates adrenalin, and that can lead to an increased libido and that can lead to..., well, you know where I'm heading. Get out there and have some fun!

25. Be Adventurous

If you are creative in the way that you approach your life, your work, and your goals, and you have a plan for the things you want to do, you will surely succeed. It's when you fall into the trap of mediocrity, the laziness of just getting by and getting over, that you compromise the quality of your life. You've got to approach your relationship and your overall life with a sense of adventure. You need a bit of not always knowing exactly what's coming next, but taking it on with excitement. Show gratitude at having the opportunity to live your best life, and creativity to make the best of every situation.

Being adventurous is about not being afraid to take the high road sometimes. That's not to say that you should destroy the structure in your schedule, by suddenly quitting your job or recklessly spending or drinking. That would be self-destructive and would likely ruin your quality of life. What I mean is think boldly. Being adventurous turns you into an optimist, someone who isn't afraid to try a new approach, take a new route, and who always expects the best from people and life. Being adventurous makes you act on living your dreams instead of just dreaming about them.

You can turn any situation into the best-case scenario if you have an adventurous mindset. It doesn't mean that you're in denial about the truth, but you refuse to be dragged down or deterred from being who you want to be. If things don't work out one way, hey, you can think of twenty other things to do instead. There's always another option, another possibility. This is a great life-skill to have and this mentality will definitely improve the quality of your relationship.

You can also get adventurous in the bedroom with your mate and try new things. This doesn't mean that you get to have a threesome and she just accepts it, or that she gets to have intercourse with another man while you watch. It's never a good idea to bring another person into your bedroom, unless you're both into that stuff. Whatever you do sexually together has to be done with extreme respect for each other's boundaries and should maintain and enhance your intimate connection.

If you practice being adventurous in general, you'll realize that those dumb, little daily annoyances that are just part of life don't affect you or disrupt your flow as much as they used to simply because you don't let them. You'll actually enjoy your life and your relationship even more.

26. Call her a sweet nick-name

Just make sure you don't embarrass her in public by calling her "Sugar Butt" or "Betty Boobs." Choose something less embarrassing along the lines of "Honey" or "Babe," "Sweetie," you know. Guys might not like to be called "Honey Bun" or "Angel Face," but they're not soft and luscious like women are. Women like to be called endearing things by their men, as long as they're sincere, complimentary and not too blatantly sexual if said in public. It let's your woman know you're into her when you call her something that no one else in her life calls her, and that you don't call anyone else in your life.

Just a Couple of Party Animals!

27. Plan a party together

This can actually be a blast. Planning a party together means letting your friends know directly and indirectly that you're serious about each other and you are having a ball with her. Make sure you both invite cool people and have a well-balanced and varied guest list. Don't invite uptight troublemakers or angry drunks. If one of you has more friends than the other, don't worry about it. Just make sure you have plenty of food, great music and drinks to cover everyone there. Then make sure the two of you enjoy yourselves too. Don't let her do all the work or play maid all night while you chill with your friends. Make sure the food and drinks are served and then take pleasure in being together with your close friends. There's a definite connection that comes from working on something social with your partner and having a good outcome. This will bring you to another level of intimacy.

28. Take her dancing

Most women love dancing!! It's a chance to release that energy while being all dressed up and shake your groove thing in front of other people. It's just a joy to dance to music you love with someone you love! It is such a turn-on for a woman to move her body to the music with a man she's in love with! Her pulse races, her adrenalin pumps, and she starts to get very hot! Why not be the object of all that good stuff!! People are going to want to see what it's all about. Focus on each other. Get into each other and tear up that dance floor. Have a great time. It's a serious aphrodisiac, and a good workout too. When you're done on the dance floor, you'll be happy to go home and tango in the sheets!

29. Learn to dance

Now you know we like to go dancing. So what's hotter than that? Dancing with a man who really knows what he's doing! We don't expect our guy to be a professional ballroom dancer or a hip hop, b-boy king. But if you can put it on her on the dance floor you're likely to start a fire. Maybe you can sign up together to learn a dance that's new to both of you, like Rhumba or Mambo (aka Salsa). Dancing causes a rush of adrenaline and a release of endorphins that is good for your psyche and your sex life. Learning to dance also gives you more confidence and something fun to work towards. The heat caused by dancing in tune with each other on the dance floor will help keep you dancing together through life.

SOUL FOOD

30. *Buy her a good book*

Book stores are usually full of people sitting around reading. Personally, a book store excites me like a kid at a candy store! If you know your mate's reading preference or she's mentioned a book she'd like to read, go and get it for her. It doesn't matter if you hate everything she reads – buy it with her taste in mind. She'll love that! If you don't know exactly what she hasn't read yet, take her to the bookstore and tell her to pick a book she's been wanting to read. She'll love that even more!

Either way, you are nurturing her mind and buying her a present at the same time, and if you go with her to get it, you're also spending time together doing yet another thing as a couple. The more you know and accept each other's tastes and styles, the tighter your bond will become. Triple points for you!

31. *Buy her coffee and a magazine*

Women love to drink something warm and delicious while flipping through a magazine looking at the latest fashion or reading up on their favorite subjects. As her man, you should learn what she's into and indulge her in it every once in a while. This is a fun Sunday morning activity and she'll appreciate it and kiss you for it. It's simple, yet indulgent. The message you're sending her is "Here hon, relax, stay inside while I take care of you this time. I know what you like." Again, when our men indulge us with things we routinely do for ourselves, it becomes a little pampering treat from him to us and we love that. Muah!

All In The Family

32. Invite her to know your family and friends

When you start getting into each other's families, it can be quite stressful. It's also a sign that you take each other seriously enough to bring the family into the picture. If you invite her to your family or friends for a dinner or other occasion, make sure you take care of her the whole time you're there. Don't forget that it could be awkward and nerve-racking for her because she's trying to make a good impression and fit in with them. Courtesy and caring are what she needs from you. You'll also train your family and show them how important this woman is to you by how you treat her around them.

You don't have to prove yourself to them; they already know you and love you. But you do have to prove yourself to her. Prove to her that you are loyal to her and are looking out for her even in the comfort (or discomfort as the case may be) of your family. You brought her there. It's your job to shield her from any awkward or embarrassing questions in an easy-going, light way that keeps the atmosphere friendly, and support her while she tries to hold her own and have a good time. She'll remember how well you treated her at your family's house and she'll take care of you too when the time comes. That's how you cross that big bridge gracefully.

Her Personal Sugar Daddy

33. Put your money where your mouth is

This again goes along with taking care of both of you. It's not something every guy is in a position to do. Remember, this is a book about ways to please your woman. I'm not suggesting you attach yourself to a useless gold-digger who eats you out of house and home and spends your money like water, unless you're into that kind of thing. It's not something you have to make a habit of either, but say you surprise her in late November and tell her you'll pay her living expenses for December. Or how about just picking up her dry cleaning, laundry or cell phone bills every once in a while. Do it on her birthday month so she can treat herself to whatever she wants or so she can catch up on some other bills or plans. Pay for her bi-weekly mani-pedi appointments – that's a really nice move that's pretty affordable. When our men encourage us to keep up with our grooming by offering to pay for it, it tells us two things: One, he loves that we take care of ourselves, and two, he's willing to help us keep it up. Plus, her fingers and toes will be ready for you to nibble on at all times.

A self-sufficient woman does not want to feel kept, and most women don't need a man's money at all. But if it's done right, these treats are highly appreciated. It's a very thoughtful and personal gesture that lets her know you're serious about her and you've put your money where your heart is. Women love a thoughtful and generous man!! Muah! Thank you baby!

Friendship First!

34. *Be her best friend*

This is so important and romantic! A serious bond of friendship is what endures through the hard times and the low points in life that everyone goes through. One of the biggest causes of relationship breakups is that couples don't really like each other outside of the bedroom or outside of their 'dating' life. You can't just date someone because she's hot, though sexual attraction is definitely of major importance. But aside from sexual chemistry, you've got to like being around each other. You've got to have other things in common that you like to do and talk about. Friends like to hang out, talk, play, eat together, laugh, etc.... If you remember to treat each other as great friends do, you'll respect each other a lot more and you won't be needy, obsessive or smothering. And most of all, you'll have fun when you're together.

That's the whole point of being in a relationship – sharing the moments of your life with someone you love to be around, and making your journey through life that much more exciting and enjoyable. So many women don't do things with their husbands because 'he's not into that' or 'that's not his thing.' They end up going to functions alone, and doing a whole bunch of activities with people other than their mate.

The more things a couple can do as friends, the closer they will be. Interacting as friends will make your bond tighter, just as not interacting as friends will bring you farther away from each other and closer to other people. If you can be her really good friend she'll trust you even more with her heart and her happiness, and you'll have much better sex, better kissing, better conversations and a better bond.

You can't and shouldn't try to replace her best female friend or her sister, but you should be the closest male relationship she has (totally different from her brothers and father – don't compete with them either!). And the same goes for her as well. There should be things between the two of you – including sex – that you don't share with anyone else, things that are just for the two of you to know. Don't try to force your way into her friendship circle, but take an active part in being there for her, like a good friend should. She'll love that!

The Way To Her Heart...

35. Be thoughtful and attentive

Remember her birthday, celebrate her promotion, take care of her when she's sick, run errands with her, pick up the dry cleaning, put the lid down in the bathroom, etc.... There are a million ways you can be thoughtful and attentive. Hold her hand when you're walking outside – don't wait for her to reach for yours. Walk at her pace; don't make her gallop to keep up with you. Fix the shelf before she asks. Walk her dog for her on winter mornings (and be damned careful with her furball!), or take her and the pooch for a nice walk in the evenings. Ask her if she's had enough to eat, if she'd like some tea, etc...

Many strong and independent women will only ask for help with something they absolutely can't do by themselves, like opening a really stuck jar of sauce, or moving a big piece of furniture. Every woman's lifestyle is different, but there's always something you can do to show her you're thinking of her at any particular moment. You don't have to and shouldn't act like her little lap dog, but when you do some of those everyday, mundane things for her, she'll appreciate you even more.

36. Take her shopping!

Okay, we know men love sex, food, sports, cars and beer. Women love sex, food, shopping, shoes, shoe-shopping, eating out, and did I mention shopping?! Take your woman to shop for something specific. Remember she's a pro, so you might not be able to hang on a full-out spree unless you're a pro shopper yourself. Keep it specific and you'll be fine. Or, make a day of it and take both of you shopping. You can hit Macy's or Sak's, Nordstrom's or Bloomie's, or some other big store where you can both go nuts. Or hit the mall and shop til you drop!

If you offer to pay for it, make sure it's within your budget. Whether you have a limit of $50, $100, $500, $1,500, or $50,000, be clear on it, but also keep it fun. Surprise her when she wasn't expecting anything. Ask her if she can go with you to help you pick something out, and then buy both of you something nice. Those are the best surprises.

If you can't afford anything at all, then don't offer this, plain and simple. That would be putting your big foot in it for sure, because women really love shopping and take an offer like that seriously. If you absolutely hate the idea of going with her, surprise her with a gift card and send her off with her girlfriends. However you share this with her, the key thing to remember is make it fun! She'll love you even more and be very grateful later.

ROCK STEADY

37. *Be level-headed and calm*

No one can deal with a hot-head, macho, madman for too long. Dating a man who's ready to pounce and explode violently is too stressful and can often be dangerous. Women appreciate a man who can handle difficult or unexpected situations with intelligence and reason. Men don't always show their emotions, but usually they're very quick to go nuts at any little situation, like someone cutting them off on the highway, or some guy staring them down at a bar.

You have to stay calm and think smart always, especially when you're out in public. I'm not telling you to suppress your emotions or repress your anger. I'm saying be careful how you channel it. You don't want to develop into a angry reactor who is always flying off the handle. You could put yourself and your woman in danger. When you're busy having a huge reaction to something, you can be missing something really important like a psycho coming at you with a pipe or a gun. If you maintain a level head you'll be able to make smarter decisions when they are most needed and you'll likely be the one walking away safe and sound from any situation you may find yourself in.

And during those occasions when you will surely encounter a hot-tempered, loud-mouthed idiot, your level-headedness will help you handle the situation like a mature, civilized man who knows how to keep things from getting ugly. Not that you can't go there, but why waste your energy needlessly. Women admire and respect a man who knows how to handle himself without violence. She feels safe with him and sees him as sexy. This is a win, win on every level.

How Can You Be There For Her?

38. Be emotionally supportive

This is a tough one, but not impossible. Being emotionally supportive simply means talking about whatever comes up in each other's lives. Men may not feel the need to do this, but it is necessary. Women often feel like they are not emotionally supported or connected in their relationships because the men don't ever ask them anything personal. Or men are so self-absorbed, aloof or disinterested that a woman wouldn't even consider going to him if she really needed some good advice because she doesn't think he'd care or could give her the kind of soothing and intelligent answers she needed to hear. So she'll go to her girlfriends or her sisters and may end up being more connected to people other than her man.

Men tend to focus on outcome. Women focus on both details and outcome. So, it's important that you share her journey with her, not just wait until she gets there. I'm speaking figuratively. The journey is whatever is going on – preparing for a test, working a job, planning a party, going through a crisis, or whatever. We want our men in our day-to-day lives, not just the big moments. Ask her how she's doing. If you know there are things going on in her life – either a stressful job, a tough class, a family issue, or what have you, ask her to talk about it and really take the time to get emotionally involved in it as her supporter.

You don't have to agree with how she's handling things, but be sensitive and open-minded. You also don't have to solve the issue for her, although if you have a brilliant solution, by all means, do tell. Maybe you can give her a different perspective on things that could help her get a resolution sooner. Just don't judge, criticize or condescend even if you don't see things her way. Listen and respond without driving her away.

Whatever it is, she should be able to share it with you if she wants to. That's part of being very close friends, and that's what serious relationships are all about. You learn to deal with whatever comes up, good and bad, as partners. She'll appreciate that you really care and are sensitive enough to take the time to listen and offer her emotional support.

39. Accompany her to her family functions and behave

We know this can be tough sometimes and uncomfortable on both sides.

It's extremely personal. But guess what? This is part of growing up together. There comes a time when you've got to get into the family if you're going to be in her life. Hopefully they're easy to get along with. Either way, you have to remember who you're in a relationship with. If she has to deal with her family and you're going to deal with her, then you've got to deal with them to some extent as well. Make the best of things. Give them a fair chance and a good attitude. Present the best of you and see how it goes. Hopefully they'll treat you with the courtesy and warmth that you show them and you'll end up getting along great.

She's the reason you're doing it and she's the one who will thank you most. Plus, if she's 'The One,' you're going to see these people again and again. The more you get along with them, the easier things will be for you and your woman going forward, where family members are concerned.

AVANTE-GARDE

40. *Be a forward-thinking man with a sense of tradition*

We have no choice but to enjoy living in the modern world – this is the world we were born into. Our only real choice is to succeed or not. As women, it's great that we live in a world where we have more choices than just getting married and having babies. We have our own lives and make our own decisions, and have careers that just a few short decades ago were much more difficult to fathom, let alone obtain. Some men are of the mindset that since women can do everything for ourselves, they don't need to do any of the traditional stuff for us in terms of chivalry and commitment. That's just not true!

Women love many of the old fashioned, traditional values that our parents and grandparents grew up with. Like the idea of a man coming to pick us up at the door. Don't call from the car and tell us to come down, or honk when you're outside the house. Come directly to the door and and then drop us directly at our door on the way back, even if it's an apartment building. Hold our chair for us when we eat out. Make a big deal about birthdays and holidays. Ask us to dance and lead us out to the dance floor. Offer your jacket if it's chilly. Don't wait for us to ask you or start sneezing all over the place.

Those little traditional things go a long way. But don't do them because you expect to get some later! Do these nice things because you care about and you want to practice being good to us. Chivalry is one of those old traditions that will always be sexy. It's this type of good, old stuff that we want to have more of. It worked back then and it definitely works now in our fast-paced and often impersonal world. A modern man with a sense of tradition is the type of man a woman wants in her bed every night. You can be that man!

Is She On Your Mind?

41. Keep her in the loop

What I mean is, let her know you're thinking of her often and let her know what's going on with you. I don't mean bombard her with 20 calls a day or constant blackberry emails when you know she's busy at work. But if you can catch her a couple of times during the day, that's always fun. Let her know what you're doing and where you are. Call her at least two or three times during her workday and again at night if you're not living together. Think of her in other ways and use some of the ideas mentioned earlier.

Women love attention from the man they're giving their time to. When you're serious about someone you think of them all the time anyway, so take the time to show it. You have to live life like there's no tomorrow, because tomorrow is not 100% guaranteed anyway. It's something we hope for, plan for, aim for. But we can only wait and see if it actually arrives. What would you want her last memory of you to be if either one of you were to suddenly not be around? Is there something you would have regretted not telling her today? Well go tell her!

CHILDLIKE, NOT CHILDISH!

42. Play nice

This is essential to your friendship and your long-term romance. Who do people want to be around? Usually it's people that they associate with fun and relaxation. Too many couples forget to have fun with each other. They get caught up in the daily routine of going to work, doing chores, paying the bills, taking care of the kids, etc..., and they end up taking each other for granted just doing grunt work. Or they are just not a good match and they never really played together, got together for the wrong reasons, and won't ever have any fun. Then they want to get away from each other to hang with their 'friends' in order to relax and have some fun. I'm not saying you shouldn't have friends outside of your relationship, but you shouldn't think of each other as 'not a friend' or 'not fun.'

If you remember to have fun with each other and play together, you'll associate fun with your relationship and you'll want to spend more quality time together after doing all the necessary, day-to-day stuff. It seems like a no-brainer, but a lot of people have problems hanging out together, and their relationship usually goes downhill. It becomes more of mundane, roommate-like coexistence and the romance goes out the window. Go play tennis, go skating, swimming, running, rock-wall climbing, shoot some hoops. Just get out of the house and do something that makes you sweat and enjoy a little friendly competition and physical exertion. Or team up and play with other couples. Playing together really helps solidify the feeling of being on a team of two, which is essentially what you are.

Live in The Moment!

43. *Be spontaneous*

Most professionals live such regimented lives that our whole year is completely divided into half-hour blocks of time. Many of us have very predictable and almost robotic schedules. A romance with a great match offers you a chance to throw a fork in your routine and remember what living is all about. Use your new adventurous energy to take a chance and put some serious excitement back in the mix. I don't mean to just cut out of your responsibilities at work and risk getting fired, but do something different every once in a while. Call her up and leave work early. Go home early on a Tuesday and go out to dinner. Take a Friday off once in a while and run away somewhere or stay in bed all weekend. There are a million ways to shake things up in a fun way for both of you. Spontaneity is a great little burst of energy that keeps things from falling into a boring, old rut. Shake things up in a good way - keep it hot!

44. *Take her to a live show*

Live is the way to go with most women. I happen to love sports, but only if I can watch them live. There is nothing like first-hand action. Women are touchy, feely creatures by nature, and that's a good thing. So we really appreciate that live experience. Take her to see something like a live play or a musical. Take her to a boxing match (unless you know she hates it). Take her to one of those restaurants where the chef cooks the food right in front of you. Go to the zoo and see real animals interacting. Take her to a tennis match, baseball game or a horse race. There's excitement that you can only feel when you're there. It's just not the same when it's coming through the tube. Live action titillates the senses and gives you a rush that stays with you. It's much better to be there live than to spend more time in front of the television. Just check the weather forecast before heading out so that you actually enjoy yourselves!

DOES HE KNOW ME OR WHAT?!

45. *Buy her some delicious chocolate*

Mmmmm, yum-my! I know you've heard about the effect chocolate has on women. It's a natural aphrodisiac and we love it! When you know what your woman likes and you get it right – you get major points! I would suggest getting her some chocolate a couple of times a year and make sure it's really delicious and imported so she can think of you every time she pops a scrumptious morsel into her mouth. If you're lucky she might share them with you or let you watch her indulge. Make sure she's into chocolate – there are actually a couple of women in the world who hate it, though I personally have never met one!

Be A Ride or Die Dude

46. Through thick and thin

This surpasses the material and financial. Though certainly a man should want to be a caretaker of his woman in some sense, even if they both have to work. He should want to make sure she's well-fed and well-dressed and emotionally happy and healthy, and financially set. I don't mean he has to tell her how to do all those things, but he should care about her well-being and happiness with more than just lip service. When a woman thinks of a man taking care of her, it's not necessarily in the way that say, a father takes care of a child. It's more about her knowing and feeling that her man's got her back no matter what. That's a huge commitment that two people make to each other, and it's usually way before there is any talk of rings or marriage. It's that feeling and that reality that separates a serious relationship from a temporary, frivolous fling.

Certainly if you're already married, hopefully you have this unbreakable connection with your mate. If you don't, it's something beautiful to work on. There is nothing like knowing that if you broke your back tomorrow, there is at least one person in this world who would be there with you to make sure you're taken care of in every way. When that person is your mate it's an amazing feeling of contentment and security.

Becoming a strong team has to start with a strong desire to be on that team. It is both wanting to be and accepting that you're a unit of two and you have to be there for each other through thick and thin. The hard work is in keeping things fun rather than tiresome. As the man in a relationship, you have to take the lead and take care of your woman. And she, being the great reciprocator, will take care of you right back.

YOU'RE THE REAL PRIZE

47. Let her win

Some guys are so competitive they often get into heated arguments just because they refuse to lose a battle. If you're one of those guys, you could be arguing over the dumbest thing and then it gets ugly and causes real damage to your relationship. You have to ask yourself what's more important, to win right now, or to keep her happy and keep the peace in the house. Again, I'm not talking about putting up with a bully who throws spoiled tantrums or verbally abuses you. But don't you be a tantrum-throwing bully-toddler either.

A good relationship involves compromising on the little, everyday stuff, and giving and taking. If you focus on keeping things positive and flowing in the right direction, you'll be mature enough to stay away from dumb debates with your woman. You can have those with your boys and compete to the finish, but keep them away from your relationship with her. Your conversations are directly related to how she feels about you physically at that moment and possibly later. Hint, hint.

48. Support her when she's down

Be her shoulder to cry on. Yes, we all want to think of ourselves and the people we date as resilient pillars of strength and independence who can take care of themselves completely on their own. Hopefully that is the case most of the time. But every now and then life throws us a curve ball that knocks us completely off balance. As her partner, you should have her back at all times – during prosperity and famine. And again, I'm talking about a person you want to be serious with and grow with.

It's easy to celebrate success – it's all fun and games at that point. But it's just as important to be there when she's down in the trenches and fighting an uphill battle or working her way out of a hole, regardless of whether it's emotional, financial, or physical. You should not be a fair-weather mate who runs and hides at the first sign of trouble. You also shouldn't be someone she doesn't feel comfortable sharing her whole truth with – someone who she has to give the edited version to for fear of being judged too harshly. Don't think she's purposely trying to complicate or add pressure to your life when she shares something difficult with you. Instead, be a good friend. Listen and support her through it. The bond you forge during her low moments will carry you through if ever the shoe is on the other foot – yours.

Imply ALL women are givers. Not true!!!

A LITTLE APPRECIATION GOES A LONG WAY!!

49. Show Her What She Means To You

This was a very important point on the lists of happy, committed couples. I want this one to really stay in the forefront of your mind! A woman likes to feel that the special man in her life knows she's the bomb! Women give, give, give; we go above and beyond what we should have energy to do just so you'll notice how special we think you are. And, yes, we want you to reciprocate! We would love it if you did a few things without us having to ask you – a few times per week. For example, if you live together or spend a lot of time at her place you can set the table, get up and do the dishes at the end of a dinner party at your house, pick up your own stuff off the floor, buy her flowers or tickets to a show she loves (even if you would rather eat glass than sit through a musical), or any number of other things she loves.

One of the secrets of successful relationships is that both partners go out of their way to make the other happy. You are not always going to like the same things and you might hate some of the things your partner loves, but if you love your partner, you have to indulge her sometimes. She will feel so appreciated and loved – it's another win-win.

On the flip side, a woman who does not feel appreciated by her mate will become increasingly frustrated, creating major arguments out of thin air. A woman will ask her mate to do several little things that she wishes she didn't have to ask, like "Did you take out the garbage?" "Why do you leave your shoes in the middle of the living room every day?" "Do you think stuff just picks itself up?" "Can you help me clean up before the guests arrive?" The list can go on and on and on, and I'm sure many of you are familiar with that tone of voice. Men call this nagging and they claim to hate it. Somehow it seems to hit an angry "I'm-being-bossed-around-and-nagged-by-my-mother" button in them, and it makes them want to argue that they're adults and can do and say whatever they want whenever they want. This doesn't usually end well. When a woman starts asking a man to do things in 'that voice,' it's probably a sign that she is frustrated about something lacking in the relationship. For example, she'll speak on the little tasks around that house that are being neglected to avoid saying how neglected or unloved she's feeling by her mate.

Women love when their men think of them, and the less time they have to spend asking for dumb, little things to get done, or wishing to be treated with some forethought and consideration, the better the relationship will be. If you already feel like you make all the gestures of appreciation, that's great. What you could do then is ask you woman, "Honey, do you know how much I appreciate you?" "Do you know how grateful I am for all the work you put into our relationship?" "You're the best." She'll really appreciate that. It doesn't take much effort to keep the vibe of your romance fresh and positive.

50. Pray together

Spirituality and religion are on the 'Big Seven' list that I discussed earlier. You can't get much more personal than praying together. It's one of those things you have to agree on before proceeding with a serious relationship because it will cause severe conflicts otherwise. If you belong to a religious or spiritual group or pray on your own and you're in a serious relationship, invite your woman to share this part of your life with you. I don't just mean blessing the meal at home either, although that could be a start. You should introduce her to that part of your life and to the people in your spiritual community. Don't force the issue if she's not ready, but don't lock her out either. It's likely that you share similar beliefs already, so this will just help solidify your connection and your understanding of each other.

Maybe you can explore your spirituality or a new belief system together to figure out what you both want to learn more about. Part of growing together is being able to share your authentic self. This is a hugely intimate gesture and will let her know just how serious you are about her. It's a beautiful thing.

PART III – TRÈS ROMANTIQUE

Good, Old-Fashioned Romance Still Works!

51. *Be Mr. Romantic*

This is why women want to be in relationships in the first place. Let's face it. If we only wanted sex or some company, we could find a million candidates who would willingly jump at the opportunity for no strings sex, and we can get a pet goldfish or a cat for companionship. What we crave in a relationship is that euphoria, that magic, that high that comes from being with the guy that gives us butterflies at the mere mention of his name. We love that feeling of heat in the nether regions of our torso at the memory of one of our evenings together, or at the thought of what is to come in the near future.

Romantic men know that her sexual attraction is directly related to how special they make a woman feel. If a woman is into a man and he knows how to pour on the romance, oh boy is he in for some fun times and fast rides. Romance is a serious turn on for women, and men reap the benefits of the euphoria that comes from feeling the closeness and physical attraction to their heart's desire. The main reasons guys tend to shy away from "being romantic" are a) they're lazy, b) they're afraid of being called corny – afraid of that rejection, and c) they have no clue how to be romantic.

Because we live in such a hit it and split time, men and women have forgotten what romance is. Many guys have wasted their time with women who weren't really interested in them. When they finally meet a great match who does want to know them and grow something special, they often forget to do those wonderful things that keep couples intertwined. Well don't be afraid. If you feel something real for your woman or you'd like to, and she's in a monogamous, exclusive relationship with you, you need to go for it. She's worth the effort. You'll feel like a teenager again. With all the adrenaline and endorphins flowing you just might start bumping like bunnies!

One of the great things about being an adult is the ability to do pretty much whatever you want. Why not live out some of those romantic fantasies you dreamed up as a teenager when you first discovered girls? Add some whimsy and fun to your life by sharing romantic moments with the woman you want to be with. She'll love it. You'll reap the rewards and both of you will have a longer, happier life together. Following are a bunch of romantic things you can do to keep her heart melting and your hormones racing.

52. *Buy her flowers*

Yes, it sounds like an old-fashioned notion or some romantic cliché, but it still works. When it comes to chivalry and romance, old-fashioned is good! Flowers are beautiful and women love getting them, seeing them, smelling them. They are visual and aromatic mood lifters and whoever can take credit for providing that pleasure is going to instantly be remembered with a smile.

We buy them for ourselves and for our family and friends, and we absolutely love getting them from our men. It tells us he's thinking of us, he wants to make us smile and makes us feel cherished and pretty. It's not something that needs to be done constantly but at least once or twice a month would be very nice. Attach a little note that says something romantic or naughty, but not trashy. "Beautiful flowers for a true beauty," or, "I'm thinking of you and smiling," or, "Can't wait to see you again." You can think of something that works for you.

Remember, all women have an inner girl who likes to be treated like a princess and if she gets that treatment from her special man, he'll be that much more special to her. It doesn't have to be a whole bouquet or even expensive. One giant sunflower is gorgeous on it's own. Two perfect pink roses are beautiful. As long as they're fresh and vibrant and you thought of it – that's what matters. She'll have you on the brain and be too busy to give her attention to your competition. She'll feel like she's got something solid with someone who remembers her and does little things just to make her smile. The more you think about each other, the more solid your connection will be. The more solid your connection, the more you'll want to be together.

53. Leave her love notes

You don't have to turn into Alfalfa from "The Little Rascals" and write one of those "Dear Darla" letters. Just a note on her pillow in the morning, or a text message on her phone telling her she's beautiful or that you can't wait to see her again will touch her heart and warm her insides. Of course, you can get her a card with flowers or a heart on it, or a postcard of some place you've gone together or would like to go with her. Alternate between sweet, little notes, and erotic, little notes (but not too vulgar). Just say something like, "You're beautiful and I want you!" or "Good morning doll – you're delicious!" Leave something to the imagination or recall a good memory.... Remember, all the little things count. The more sparks you can add to your fire, the hotter your romance will be.

IT'S THE LITTLE THINGS...

54. Take her on a lunch date

It is so much fun to have a mid-day rendezvous with your love interest every once in a while. It could be something as simple as grabbing some Chinese food at the local spot close to the office, or a quick picnic at the park. If you're really adventurous, rent a hotel room for a few hours or race home and kidnap each other for the rest of the afternoon.

Escaping for a quick lunch as a couple is not only romantic, but it's intoxicating. It builds intimacy between you and establishes that flash of energy between you that is special and thrilling. This is a great way to stay connected and keep things sizzling! Keep your love affair crackling with the sparks of desire. Have a new and exciting lunch date with your woman once a week or so.

55. Kiss frequently and deeply

Kissing is so important and sensuous – it's romantic, hot, wonderful and very necessary. It is such an intimate gesture. If you have a partner to kiss, you should spend as much time doing it as possible. This one should be in all the sections of this book because it is a necessary basic, sweet and romantic, super hot and a definite part of the total package. A kiss has the power to make or break an evening and a relationship.

Kiss her hello and goodbye – everytime. When you're out on a date – kiss her every so often to keep those lips warm. When you're alone, start out kissing her slowly and lightly, but get more intense and kiss different body parts. Our bodies are full of erogenous zones - finger tips, inside of the wrist, the neck, the collar bone, the hip bone, the back of the knees, the arch of the foot, earlobes, and on and on. Find all her spots and take your pick! Kisses are an instant turn on.

If you don't kiss your partner it spells doom for your relationship. That would be like a hungry bear ignoring a juicy salmon; it's just unnatural. You can make your woman go totally over the edge with the right kind of kissing. She'll get so hot and bothered, soon you'll both be in a frenzy and hopefully end up happily exhausted.

56. Bring her breakfast in bed

This is really romantic, and is preferable on a weekend when you're both off and don't have to run out early. Make her some of her favorites, or grab some quick stuff like juice, fruit, toast and cereal. If she's a heavy sleeper, you have time to get up and cook a more gourmet breakfast – pancakes or french toast, scrambled eggs, home fries and fresh coffee or tea. If she's a light sleeper, she's likely to get up right behind you, so you have to be quick. Coax her back to bed if she gets up, or opt to eat on the living room floor – it still counts. The whole idea is to spend some quality time in the morning and show her you want to satisfy all her senses. It's very likely you'll finish up breakfast with dessert – in bed. This is a great way to start the weekend!

TAKE IT UP A NOTCH!

57. Plan a Weekend Getaway

Most women love to travel and escape, even for a weekend. What more romantic gesture can there be than for a man to plan a getaway with his woman? Women are planners; we make lists, buy tickets, and even plan the whole year sometimes. So it's really nice when a man takes care of the arrangements and does so with his woman in mind. This doesn't have to be expensive or even involve taking the Friday or Monday off, although the longer the weekend, the better. Even an overnight trip is fun if it's not too far. You can go straight after work and be back by Sunday night. If you're really good, you'll plan it around your work holidays when you're both off on Monday. We love the idea of going somewhere and being together, just the two of us. The overnight aspect is sexy and intriguing because it means we'll likely spend the night between the sheets and wake up together in a new place.

Make sure you plan well, go someplace you will both enjoy and that she will love. Make sure it's within your budget, and make sure you're both healthy at the time. Weekend getaways are adventures that should take place at least once a month or once every two months. This will score you some major points and will hopefully add a lot more sizzle to your fire.

58. Draw her a rose bath

I'm not talking about your regular, everyday, run-of-the-mill, hot bath with bubbles and Epsom salts. That kind will show up later on this list. I'm talking about the bath full of very warm water, some buttermilk or heavy cream (make sure she's not allergic to dairy!), honey, bath salts, and topped off with rose petals and a little jasmine oil for fragrance (If you can't find jasmine or lavender oil, just light a scented candle. Try to keep her entertained in the living room while you prepare everything. Then place different sized candles all around the bathroom (in safe places – don't burn the house down!), and create a rose petal path from the hallway or the bedroom, all the way to the bathtub. Have some of your favorite slow songs playing softly (far, far away from the water!!), and have a robe laid out on the bed for her. Be prepared to let her enjoy it by herself. Undress her slowly in the bedroom and kiss her shoulders and collar bone. Then put the robe on her (yes, you have to show restraint!), and hand her a glass of champagne with a sweet strawberry inside and tell her to follow the path to the bathroom. She will instantly start to relax and feel extremely loved and appreciated!! Here's what she'll probably be thinking – "I am so lucky! What a wonderful man I have! I'm going to do something nice for him." Keep that love energy flowing and it reflects right back on you.

Turn on the Charm, Baby!

59. *Have a candle lit dinner for two*

If you cook it yourself and it turns out delicious, that's extra romance points for you. Women do love a man who can cook! But if you are completely inept in the kitchen, you can have it delivered from a great restaurant. It doesn't have to be expensive, but it does have to be delicious and you should pick foods you know she loves. Many of the best restaurants don't deliver, so plan on picking the food up and having a way to keep it warm.

Set a lovely table, with flowers and candles and soft music. Maybe have a bottle of wine or champagne and a single rose on the table. If you have a fireplace, move to the floor and set up a low table or a blanket with placemats for the food and cushions for you both. There's something about soft candle light that creates a romantic mood, and definitely cranks the heat up. A delicious, romantic meal in cozy surroundings is a wonderful prelude to a lovely evening.

60. *Sing her a song*

Play it on your guitar, your piano or your horn (the other horn) or your timbales. Whatever musical talent you've got is a plus for you. Even if you sound like a dying goat and she ends up laughing hysterically, she'll think it's the sweetest thing, so sing away! Make sure it's something romantic that expresses something about the way you feel about her. Start dancing and singing, "The Way You

Make Me Feel," by Michael Jackson and go all out. Sing a Bob Marley song in her ear while you're out in public. That is so romantic and creates such intimacy between you because there are people around but it's still all about the two of you. Music is an aphrodisiac to many and it has the power to connect people across miles of oceans and seas. Imagine what it can do for your relationship. Work it!

SUBTLETY WORKS TOO!

61. Pretend to read her palm

Okay, so this is a way for you to do two things: get her hand in yours and feel it, and conveniently read her into your future. Look at her palm and find her lifeline, her heart line, her love line, etc…, and make a big deal of noticing that you have the same line on your hand even if you don't. You'll be sending her the message that you're thinking of the future and you'd like her to be in yours. Then turn her palm over and kiss the back of her hand. Turn it back over and kiss her palm and then the inside of her wrist. This is considered a very romantic and intimate gesture in certain cultures, and it also sparks nerve endings in the hand and all the way up the arm. It will hopefully lead to more kissing.

This One's Especially For My Baby!

62. Plan a surprise party for her

Most people love good surprises – the key words are *good surprises.* Celebrate her birthday, her graduation, promotion, new job, anything! Just make her the center of the party and keep it hushed until it happens. If you absolutely know for a fact that she would rather eat dirt than have a surprise party, opt to include her in the planning of her own party, but still make it special. It is wonderful to have the man you care about think about you enough to plan a party in your honor. Imagine how special she'll feel knowing that the man she loves can pull this off! All the guys I know who have done this are very happy men in strong, satisfying relationships. That's good to know.

63. Whisper in her ear

Women love this if you tell her something sweet and funny. This is especially effective in public. Women love PDAs, but not the vulgar, slobber-her-down, feels-like-she's-making-out-with-Feely-the-Octopus type. Decorum is definitely a good thing, but that doesn't mean you should treat her like a stranger in public. Remember, intimacy happens with little things that you do that are exclusively between the two of you, even in public.

64. Look deep into her eyes

You'll probably make her blush, and that's a good thing. Try to get her to see what you feel for her by the way you look at her. Again, if you do this in public it's even better, but do it in private too. The eyes are mirrors to the soul. This is not a substitute for expressing your feelings verbally, but it is an intimacy builder that will bring a smile to her lips and possibly some heat to other areas. It's a serious turn on.

65. Go for long walks hand in hand

This is a great way to get to know each other. Walking and talking is what friends do, so why not do it with your mate? Find a great park or scenic part of town and enjoy a stroll while holding hands and chatting about everything or nothing. Just enjoy each other's company and presence while you take in the view outside. Throw in a few kisses and hugs while you're at it.

GET YOUR MOJO ON!!

66. Candles, Incense, Music

These are great mood setters. If you live together, this is a great way to wind down after a long, stressful day at work. If you're dating, this is great with dinner or after dinner with drinks and dessert. If you have a fireplace, all the better. Pick scents and smells that you both like – remember, there are two people in the relationship and you're learning to share your lives and your likes.

67. Slow Dance

Remember when you were a young teen and you couldn't wait to dance with that pretty girl you had a crush on? Well, now you can dance with that pretty girl you have a crush on who's in your life. Slow dancing is a serious aphrodisiac if you get all into it. Many women love to dance because it involves music, moving and touching. A man who indulges his woman in slow dancing might cause some serious heat to rise between them, and you know where that leads. You don't even need dancing ability to slow dance. Just find some great music you both love and hold on tight.

68. Hold her close at night

This is so important! Women need to be held, especially after making love at night or in the afternoon or morning, basically whenever you are intimate. This is a scientific fact; you can look it up. Being held in the right way and touched lovingly after lovemaking gives a woman that afterglow that her man better lay claim to. The more endorphins and serotonin you cause to course through her body, the more she'll want your body nearby. Cradle her in your arms and tell her how beautiful she is. Hopefully you can fall asleep and wake up that way. If you start to lose feeling in your arms, by all means change positions, but keep a hand on her and try to hold her again before she wakes up.

Your woman feels vulnerable after making love. She just opened her whole self up to you, literally and figuratively. That's really a gift. Especially in this world of hump and jump and often meaningless sex. It's important that you acknowledge the importance of what she is giving you and make her understand that you get it. It's your job to turn that vulnerable feeling into a happy and secure glow. If you're in love with this woman, you should want to do this. And it's actually important for you to do this for her. If this is something you hate doing, maybe it's time for you to reevaluate your fear of intimacy or perhaps your choice of partner. Holding her close and telling her she is beautiful is the way to get closer and keep her into you by staying on her mind.

Wine & Dine Her!

69. Take her out often

Going out on dates is a must for a woman. She loves to be out, be seen, and feel special. From birth to adulthood, girls love to play dress up. It is a turn on and instant adrenaline rush for a woman to have someplace to go and dress the part. If you want to keep her close to you and into you, be the one that she has fun partying with. Plan formal outings like a concert or a dance show a couple of times a year. Take her dancing once a month and to as many parties as possible , especially during the holidays, when dressing up is usually the norm. Get all dressed up and take her on a dinner date – just the two of you. Or invite a few other couples and make a night of eating, drinking, dancing and coming home happy and excited to be alone at last. More casual daytime outings are great too. Go see a baseball game or play softball with friends, take in a new exhibit at the museum, stop by an aquarium after lunch, take her for a golf lesson, or go sailing.

Spending time out with just each other or with a group of good friends will keep things exciting. There are a million things you can find to do together if you just think and plan. Hanging out in various settings is not only fun, but will help you both grow as individuals and as friends. The dressing up will add another dimension to your life as a couple and increase your attraction and desire for each other.

Diamonds Are a Girl's Best Friend

70. Buy her pretty, sparkly things

This is a definite winner and a serious turn on! Women love a variety of things and they really love receiving sparkly gifts. They also love to be close to the men that can provide them. It's just human nature. If you're the one she loves and also the one that gives her beautiful bling or some other love token a few times a year, she'll feel cherished and closer to you because you thought of her in such a big way. It will make a difference in your relationship. I'm not trying to encourage you to attempt to buy her love, nor am I suggesting that jewelry and clothes can compensate for a bad relationship. A man can't neglect all the other areas and just buy his free pass (although we all know people who do this). I'm also not suggesting that she won't appreciate you if you don't buy her nice things.

I'm writing under the premise that you've already chosen a great woman who cares about you deeply and whom you want to keep happy. Jewelry given under the right circumstances creates an extra spark because it's beautiful and because you thought of it. Do not give her a gift after you've pissed her off or had a serious fight. That will shift you into the wrong energy. Gifts should be given at happy times so they'll be cherished and shown off with good memories and good stories attached to them. The old 10 karat rock given to make up for getting busted with a ho doesn't fly with beautiful, quality women, and will only be taken for it's monetary value, or as in the case of one famous basketball louse, to save face under the media's ever-critical eye.

The gifts that we truly cherish are the ones given with love – like bracelets at a birthday dinner, heart necklaces on Valentine's Day, diamond earrings at an anniversary, a watch at Christmas, a gorgeous dress for a special occasion, a ring on a beautiful summer night. I'm sure you get the picture. Those are the gifts that have an impact on our hearts and our feelings for our men.

The thoughtfulness in selecting something pretty, not necessarily the price tag is what's appreciated. Beautiful things usually cost money and there's nothing wrong with spending if you can afford it, but a major splurge is not required to make that gift special. A woman usually knows what is within her man's means, and she appreciates his gesture if it's sincere and thoughtful.

SLOW YA ROLL MAN!

71. Be loving, gentle and affectionate

This is almost a no-brainer, but you'd be surprised how many guys think being affectionate means initiate quick sex. It doesn't. Women need love and affection that may or may not lead to sex. Woman want sex just as much, if not more than men. Believe it. However, women like to feel closeness before they get the urge to have sex most of the time. Or rather, they'll really enjoy sex and want it more often if they feel closer to their partner. Men tend to feel closer after having sex, and women before sex, so there is a definite discrepancy there.

If you take the time to touch your woman in loving ways and speak to her in a loving manner she'll be more physically attracted to you. Don't speak to her like you speak to your buddies with little regard for hurt feelings and sometimes no sign of manners. Speak to her and treat her like she's precious to you and someone you want to be around constantly. She'll feel more connected to you and undoubtedly think of you sexually more often. When you're waking her up after a nap or in the morning, don't just yank her leg and yell, "Hey, Wake up!" You need to be gentle and treat her like she's soft, even though she's probably very strong. Whispering or kissing her awake will have a much more positive effect on her and on you.

Guys like to use the excuse, "I have to toughen her up because people are not going to be nice to her in the real world." Well, duh! She's living in the real world too, remember? She knows what it's like out there and she'd been surviving long before you came around. You can help raise her awareness without being mean or brutish. The fact is, women don't really need men anymore the way they used to back in the day. She definitely doesn't need you to be tough with her unless you're her personal trainer.

We want you to be our respite from the big, bad world by treating us like we're a tender beauty that you want to protect and play with. We want to be hugged, cuddled, held, coddled, spoiled, etc... Rub our hair, touch our cheek, cover us with soft kisses.

When you're with your woman and you're interacting with her, be gentle. That doesn't mean turn into a wuss, mush, pansy and expect her to treat you like you're the soft, little kitten. That's rather effeminate and a major turn off for her. On the other hand it doesn't mean that you constantly have her in a yoke or treat her like an invalid while you're out in public. The occasional brush of your thumb against her fingers while you're walking and holding hands, or a kiss on her temple while you're waiting for a taxi or a table are sweet displays of affection that tell her you care and you're gentle. When you and your big, manly self – the big, macho man that she loves, are tender and loving to her, it really shows her what she means to you and she will love you for your gentleness and appreciate you time and time again.

PART IV: HOT, HOT, HOT!!

It's getting Hottttt In Here!

72. Make her purr

Being a great lover is not only hot and sexy, it's vital for a long lasting relationship. The woman in your life is already into you before you ever get to the bedroom. That's probably what makes her more important and special to you too and hopefully you are really into her outside of the bedroom as well. Okay, so you think she's hot and you want her! Hopefully you're sexually compatible and have tremendous heat between you. You can keep it going with the help of this book! This is where you get some juicy details about physical pleasure.

There are so many ways you can do this – I'll run a scenario by you. It starts of course, outside of the bedroom with some good conversation and cuddling. Your woman wants to feel like you have that connection that leads her to want more. If you say the right things sincerely, her libido can go through the roof. Unfortunately, the opposite is also true. A woman can have every intention of attacking her man, but one wrong word from him will shut the whole operation down, sometimes for good. Making a woman purr involves satisfying as many of her senses as possible, all in the same night. If you can master this, you'll be a very, very appreciated and happy man. Don't be surprised if you suddenly discover that your woman has hidden talents like cooking you a feast, or giving you excellent massages. Or maybe she'll surprise you with tickets to see your favorite team in action, or a weekend trip with your boys. When you're a good lover and your woman is purring, you turn on that love faucet in her and she'll want to do more for you and to you. So learn this lesson well! Start with the romantic list you read earlier and that will lead you to needing this list. The following are suggestions, but it's up to you to become skilled at the combination that works for your woman.

WHO'S THE MAN?

73. Be driven and ambitious

There's something about a man on a mission that drives a woman insane with desire! Your woman already respects you and is into you. When she sees that you're really about something and you still make time to include her in your life, she's going to want to be there with you even more. Don't ever give up or get lazy with your goals or your career.

A man who's going places is a man who will be able to provide an even better life for his family or future family. The woman who has this man in her life will feel blessed and proud to stand beside him and cheer him on because she'll be able to see that they have a good future ahead of them. That's what life is all about - growing, achieving, living well and sharing it with someone special.

Women want to be with a winner. A man on a mission is about something; he's the kind of frontrunner a woman wants to be with. Stay driven. It's a must, and it's sexy.

But at the end of the day
there is a timeline
and results are the only thing that
counts.

Mercury Rising...

74. Focus on her feet

You can have her levitating if you do this right!! I would suggest you start this in the bathtub and maybe keep it there as long as possible. Start with a foot massage. Work your thumbs into her arches, rub the balls of her feet and squeeze her heels gently. Start kissing her arches and insert one of her toes into your mouth. If she's ticklish, beware that she doesn't knock your head into next week by accident. It's best to hold on firmly and tell her to relax. Rub her calves while her toes are in your mouth and watch for her reactions. Kiss your way up her legs, focusing on her ankles, calves and knees. By the time you're at her inner thighs, you should hear the distinct sound of purring. Be ready to handle your business.

75. Lick and suck all her erogenous zones

My suggestion is that you focus on one area at a time, until you're a very experienced lover. Otherwise you'll just be slobbering all over her and she can get disgusted or turned off, and your tongue will get really dry or sore. Erogenous zones include but are not limited to fingers, palms, wrists (inside), earlobes, pulse points, back of neck, collar bone, upper back, small of the back, back of knees, inner thighs, hips, belly button, butt cheeks, arches of the feet, toes – almost everywhere.

You've got to go for it. The obvious ones, nipples, areolas, and vagina, should be approached indirectly from other areas for increased stimulation. This will cause lots of moaning and heat!

Create Anticipation

76. Buy her some sexy underwear

Women love presents, and hopefully she'll love your choice. Make sure you get her something that she'll love, not just something you'd love to see her in. Not all women are as adventurous or secure about their bodies, so make a wise choice that is her size, and covers areas that you know she's uncomfortable with. If she's a totally unabashed goddess, then get her whatever little feathery, leathery, lacy piece of fabric you'd like to take off of her, and only use your teeth and your tongue to remove it!

77. Take your time

We live in a very fast paced world. We're always rushing to meet some deadline or catching a train to punch a clock. When it comes to making love, women do not want to just rush right through it. We want a lover with a slow hand sometimes, like that old song says. Yes, there is a heated frenzy at times and you can go with that. But we don't want a man-sized bunny humper bumping us for all of five minutes and that's all she wrote. That's not pleasurable and can give us the female equivalent of blue balls – not a fun feeling. Take your time and savor it. Light some candles. Put on some cologne. Play a romantic cd and set the mood. Wine her, dine her. Get this heated up in another room or the bathtub. Talk for a little while. Kiss her finger tips. Kiss deeply and keep that heat by going slowly and building up.

Make love as long as possible until you're both exhausted and ready for sleep. Wake up and start again. In our fast-paced world and with our high-speed lifestyles, it's really pleasurable and healthy to take the time to get your groove on in slow motion. It makes her feel like she really matters to you when you take your time. It makes time stand still and your deep connection will get you more early morning and afternoon quickies. Purrr.

78. Feast on her like she's the most delicious dessert

There's no way around this one. I'm not trying to be vulgar, but if you've ever had great fellatio or a 'blow job' performed on you, then you've come close to experiencing the incredible pleasure a woman feels when cunnilingus is done right. The only women who say they don't enjoy or want this performed are the one's who've never had it or the ones who've never had it done properly. You should definitely do this often and practice until you get it right.

The key is slow and steady. Listen to what she wants – she'll usually guide your head with her hands or her thighs. If she starts writhing and moaning, that's generally a sign that you're doing great. Be prepared to ride it out or if she starts pulling you by the ears, that means she's ready for penetration.

If you're a bit squeamish about this, you have to get over it. I would suggest you start this in the shower and then take it to the bathroom floor or the bedroom. Put a peppermint in your mouth and let your mouth water, make sounds, get all into it. Put yourself in a position to give and receive, and she'll surely be purring with hot, hot pleasure. Savor the succulent nectar that you are eliciting from your beloved.

You have the power to take her to the brink of ecstasy, and over the edge. Why not cross the brink together? She'll look at you differently and you'll have a big, cheese grin on when she's through with you. If she's whipped because of the things you do to her, she'll definitely want to stick around for more.

79. Love her like there's no tomorrow

This is also known as tearing that ass up! This is where you go buck wild, take no prisoners, use every surface at your disposal. You have to ride her, flip her, devour her.... From the back, from the front, from the side.... It's something you build up to or sometimes, the fervent heat is there right at the beginning and you're in a frenzy all the way through. Women love this type of love making as long as they feel they have a caring and enthusiastic partner. Try to control yourself long enough for her to climax and hold on for the ride. That is key!

The point is to wear her out with your virility and skill. If you have a problem holding back, do what you have to do – Viagra, herbal supplements, etc... Speak to a professional before taking anything or applying any creams though. If your woman can have an orgasm more often than you do, she'll always want to have sex with you. It can be a real deal sealer.

Hold On, Hold Out!

80. Ladies first

So many women are short-changed in the bedroom either because they're so hot the man can't prolong his orgasm long enough for her to have one, or he has premature ejaculations because he never learned to control it. In the worse case, he doesn't think she needs to have an orgasm and he focuses only on his own. That's not nice. Don't get it twisted. Women need that release just as badly as you do.

It usually takes women longer to reach orgasm, especially in the beginning of a new relationship. Long, slow strokes that cause some friction on the vulva and clitoris usually get the job done. Long foreplay before you actually have intercourse will usually help get there faster, and once you are making love you have to resist the urge to speed up unless you can keep that pace up for 20 minutes or more, allowing time for her to climax with you or just before you. Once you figure out what works for her, you'll learn how to take her there faster.

You need to do whatever it takes to prolong your erection long enough for her to climax with pleasure as often as possible, not just every now and then. It takes discipline and caring, practice, and sometimes even toys. If you think you might have a problem, speak to a professional or find information online and get back to practicing. There are many great products like Ginseng, Horny Goat Weed, and of course, good 'ole Viagra, and others that claim to help men sustain themselves. Speak to a doctor about it before taking anything. Just don't give up! If you can help her get there, she'll keep coming back to you time after time.

Happy women have happy men who cause lots of exhausting and satisfying orgasms two to three (or more) times per week. Those happy men discover that their hot women also like to take care of them in their own unique ways. Overall, sexually satisfied couples are very content in other areas of their relationships as well.

Sexually frustrated women lose their desire to please their mates and their enthusiasm for the relationship and for life in general goes out the window. Suddenly all your little habits are really annoying to her, she's complaining all the time or worse, she's never home with you or doesn't plan things or do those special things for you like she used to. Relationships where one of the partners is sexually frustrated due to the impotence, neglect or laziness of the other partner don't usually work out.

Make sure she's taken care of. She'll think of you way more often, and you'll be happier. Work on it. Sexual connection and satisfaction is a major way to please a woman.

PART V: THE TOTAL PACKAGE

A Leader To Follow

81. Encourage her to follow her goals and live her dreams

Many times women in serious relationships and marriages put their personal goals at the end of a long list of other things that need to get done, especially if there are children in the picture. Their dreams get shoved in the closet or forgotten. This is a mistake. When they finally wake up and realize they didn't fulfill their personal goals, it may cause what is often referred to as a mid-life crisis.

As her friend and lover you should encourage your woman to talk about her goals and share her dreams with you. This is something extremely intimate and essential to our development, but often because we get side-tracked by the daily humdrum activities of life, or because we're afraid of being criticized by the people we care about, we keep our goals and desires a secret. Eventually many of those desires are just forgotten and we wake up feeling like, "Man, where did my life go? What were my dreams?" It happens to a lot of people, not just women, but women often put everyone else's needs ahead of their own, especially when they are in a committed relationship and/or have children. It seems many woman are often one of two ways: career driven workaholics who take on the men in their chosen field and battle their way through the ranks, often neglecting other areas of their lives in their single-minded pursuit of success. Or, the other side of that – women who will take 'just a job' to help pay the bills, who give up hopes of having a fulfilling career altogether in order to be there for their mate and their kids. It's a tough choice and certainly in our economic times, it's understandable. What I'm suggesting is that you can be there for the people in your life and have personal fulfillment with the support and understanding of your partner. A secure, loving partner should encourage his woman to not only share her goals, but set out to achieve them, even if it means having to juggle your time together. That might be the motivation she needs to move forward in the right direction and remain happy or change both your lives for the better.

Hopefully she'll do the same for you. That's how you grow together. You encourage each other to go forward without the fear that you'll outgrow each other or leave the other behind. When you feel supported by your mate, you find a way to make things work because that's the type of person you want in your life for the long haul.

Part of feeling like you're meant to be together, is having your life still fit and adjust while you both grow as individuals. If you both put your dreams on the 'agenda,' you can really become a well-oiled machine, a dream team of two.

The energy of two happy people supporting each other through goals and ambitions is an amazing thing to have in a household. Couples often forget to help each other work towards individual goals as part of their collective goals. Because of the nature of our society, a woman is often the one in a relationship who compromises her dreams right off the "TO DO" list. Make sure you find out your partner's dreams and see if you can't be her motivator and coach and work towards your dreams together. She will love you even more and you will have a greater chance at long-term bliss.

HUMOR + ATTRACTION = GREAT SEX!

82. *Make Her Laugh, Tap That A**!!*

Humor is essential to a great relationship. Women love a guy with a great sense of humor. It's not enough for her to make you laugh. you need to make her laugh. I'm not talking about becoming a slapstick fool, unless you have that kind of talent. But women get very turned on by a man who can make them laugh. Laughter is good for the soul and can definitely put you in the mood. A man who isn't stuffy and can make his woman laugh is a sexy man with a happy center. Laughing creates a similar feeling and reaction as listening to a great singer. There are studies that show how our serotonin and endorphin levels go up when we laugh. We get all tingly and excited and want to release some of that good stuff on the object of our affection. If the laugh-maker is also her man, a woman will probably want to pounce on him. Surveys that ask women what makes their sex lives hotter and more satisfying show that laughter in and out of the bedroom leads to more sizzle time.

POOR BABY!

83. Sympathize when she's got cramps!

Monthly cycles and childbirth are two things men should be extremely grateful they'll never experience. Since you have no clue what either of these are like, please don't make light of it, ever. Just like men are extremely sensitive when it comes to their family jewels, women are also sensitive when it comes to their bodies. Some men are horrible during a woman's worse time of the month and some are very insensitive during pregnancies. The only thing a woman wants to hear from her man with regard to her cramps or her swollen ankles or sore back is, "Can I get you anything?" "Would you like some tea?" "How about a backrub and a warm compress?" "Tylenol?" "Midol?" "A Pillow?" Nothing else. For some women there is nothing worse than the PMS that comes a week or two before their actual cycle. This is a medical condition that torments many women each month, when their hormones are out of control and they are miserable and emotionally sensitive. If your woman has this problem, hopefully she's taking something to keep her moods in check, otherwise she's just a little more delicate at that time. Other women don't have PMS at all, but they get horrible, kill-me-now cramps for two or three days every month. It's important that you are sensitive during that time because she's having a really difficult time and is just trying to make it through each day without dying.

The same rules apply for pregnancies and later on in life with menopause. There are hormonal things going on in the body during those times that women have little or no control over, and having a sensitive partner is really essential. She'll appreciate the little things you do, and if she's happier, you'll be happier too.

It's the Big, Little Things!

84. Clean up!

Whether you live together or not, a woman really appreciates a man who cleans up at least once a week. This is high on the list of things women want. We all would like our men to help out more around the house or be neater in general. If she cooks dinner for you or even if you order out, be the one to clear the mess and wash the dishes every now and then. If you're living together or married and you both work full time, or if she's a stay-at-home-mom, don't leave all the cleaning up to her. She's bushed!! Clean up the kitchen, do the floors and windows. Laundry is a big deal too. Get your clothes into the hamper instead of leaving them where they land. How about the bathroom? That's an annoying task that needs doing all the time. Maybe you can split up the chores and get them done on weeknights so your weekends are free. Hopefully you and your mate are pretty well-matched when it comes to sharing the household chores. Either way, a man who goes out of his way to clean up around the house is seen as a very thoughtful partner and a good catch. If you absolutely hate cleaning as much as she does or your schedules are impossible, splurge on a cleaning service twice a month. You get even bigger points for this because you'll both have the extra time and energy to get into more important things, like each other!

THE VIRTUES

85. *Be passionate*

What makes some guys hotter than others when they're not necessarily the best-looking guys? It's their level of passion. It's that *je ne sais quoi*, that zest and energy that they carry with them that charges the air around them with electricity. Passion is sexy. If you have a passion for what you do and have a lot of enthusiasm for life, chances are you're happy, confident and probably a willing and exciting lover too. Both you and your woman will benefit from that. Passion is the spice of life. It's contagious and magnetizing. It keeps things hot and fun. If you haven't been passionate before, find a reason to start right now. Live fully, love fully and enjoy the wild ride! That's what life is all about.

86. *Be generous*

Being giving and big-hearted involves a lot more than using your money, though that's certainly one way to show it. Be generous with your time, with your affection, with your attention, and with your love. Give your woman quality pieces of you, and your relationship will blossom and make you even happier. If you hold back and skimp on your affection, emotions, enthusiasm and lovemaking, to try to protect yourself from hurt or just taking with no giving back, you're doomed. You will get exactly what you don't want because essentially that's what you're working towards.

Give her what you've got and give her what you want more of. Be generous with your time, your love, your affection, your toys, your lovemaking, your conversation, your money (if you have it), your whole self, etc.... That's what a relationship is for, after all. It's all about sharing each other. Do it and be generous about it. It will make you grow. With the right mate and the right moves your generosity comes back to you tenfold.

87. Be patient

A good relationship requires work. Getting to know someone and getting to trust someone is work. She's going through it too, with you. She's not going to trust you right off the bat or be in love with you right at the start. You've got to build something that keeps you interested in growing and moving forward. You're both going to have habits that the other can't stand. You've both got to do that dance of give and take and bend and stretch. You've got to hang in there while you get to know her and you've got to develop a rhythm that works. It requires time, devotion, hard work and lots and lots of patience. If you've picked the right person, it's all worth it.

88. Be happy

No matter what you do, how much you give to others, how hard you work to make things great at home, if you're not happy with yourself, none of that stuff that you do or acquire is going to make you happy. A happy man is a happy partner. Most of that happiness has to come from within you. You can't rely on outside influences from things and people to give you everything you need.

Even though this book is all about how to please a woman, it's not a book that suggests you should neglect yourself in the process. You have to keep yourself happy too. That's the only way you'll want to do anything for your partner and that's the only way your relationship will grow and last. A good friend of mine was going through a difficult time in her marriage. She and her husband love each other very much and after weeks of flaring tempers, stupid arguments, with him generally being sullen and moody, he finally asked her what he could do to make it up to her. She told him, "Just do whatever you need to do to make yourself happy again, and I'll be fine. We'll be fine." I thought that was such great advice and such a mature approach to her stressful situation. She was able to see what the problem was, and instead of causing him to feel more guilt or anger or stress, she told him to take care of himself because she knew that his unhappiness was the root of the issue. He was feeling unhappy about his career, but wouldn't share his feelings with her. He was just showing her the symptoms caused by the unhappiness and insecurity he was feeling. He then decided to listen to his wife and make himself happy. He reconnected with some business contacts and got himself a new position with a promising future, and was feeling better within a few days. He took her advice and it worked. And, he was also willing to face his issue and find a solution. That effort made all the difference. They are back in a good place and enjoying their happy, busy lives.

Do you Really Trust Her?

89. Let her drive your car!!

Yes, we know how you guys feel about your driving machines! Often they are a sort of mechanical alter ego that shows the world how our men would like to be perceived. Women know how much that car means to you and if you really want to show your woman how special she is and how seriously you take her, let her drive your prized possession. If you're the kind of guy that lets anyone get behind the wheel of his vehicle, then this won't make any kind of impact on her. But if you are the kind of guy that gets as excited around fiber glass and horse power as most women get at a shoe sale, then trusting her with your 'off limits' car would be a very big show of your affection.

The car is just one example of what you can use to show her how much she means to you. You can substitute any of your special possessions to show her your trust this way. It could be a boat, an instrument, a special collection, some cherished artwork or books. If you share something that is all yours with your woman, you're sure to show her that you're ready to be in it for the long term with her. If she knows how special that possession is to you, she'll appreciate the gesture and cherish that trust.

Awww, He Loves Me!

90. Offer her your last bite

This is another one of those examples of how women think totally differently than men. Most people love food, and when it's your favorite it's really tough to give up that last bit of scrumptious flavor. A man might not think this is a big deal, but to a woman, it's definitely love when you're eating something delicious and you give her your last morsel. When you do this, you are showing her that you too can be a nurturer to her. That you love her more than that food and you're willing to give it to her because she's so special to you. Mother's often do this with their kids – they feed them off their own plates and they'll give that child every last bite if the child really wants it.

Offering her your last bite is a true sign of caring and affection that tells her she's special to you. Your woman might not even take the bite if she doesn't love that food as much as you do or has had enough, but she'll remember that you offered it and you'll be taking a small but important step towards closeness. It's that easy sometimes!

LET THE GOOD TIMES ROLL!

91. Celebrate accomplishments and create new traditions

These are two separate points, but they go hand in hand, so I'm giving you the two of them together. Yes, it's just as important to be there for the good times as it is for the bad ones. Hey, that's how you build a life with your partner – sharing the moments and creating memories together. When she achieves a goal, as when you do, you should make a huge deal about it. Too often people take each others moments for granted. Or the focus is all on the man's financial achievements.

Many women complain that while their men may speak very highly of them to their friends, they never tell them directly. And I've heard sad comments like, "I know he cares about me though." Well, guess what? She doesn't really know; she's only hoping you really care about her. She needs to hear it from you just like you need to hear it from her. She's not going to get it through osmosis. You have to tell her.

If you're proud of something your woman does, take her out to celebrate it. Use that previous idea and throw a party with friends and colleagues, or just have an intimate dinner with the two of you at a great restaurant.

Get excited about each other and you will always want to be together. Create some new traditions that include celebrating excellence and personal milestones. Knowing that there will be a special celebration upon reaching your next milestone as individuals will keep you both excited about your life together and create that special closeness that comes from sharing traditions with people you love. That uplifting vibe is infectious, and it will propel you both towards more happiness and success.

MOVE IT FORWARD!!

92. Make a wishlist for your future together

This is a great way to show her you mean business with her. When you're working on your 5-year plan, work on it with her. Jot down all the places you both would like to see, where you'd like to live, how many kids and pets you'd like to have. You get the idea. When you write down your desires and dreams for your life and your lists are intertwined, you're really taking each other seriously and formulating a plan for living the life of your dreams. Couples who can see a life together and start working towards it have a great chance of continuing to grow and move in the same direction throughout their lives.

FULL SPEED AHEAD!!

93. Propose!

I can't tell you how important this is to a woman! For most of us this is one of the big milestones in our lives. It doesn't matter what you've read elsewhere. This is one of those unanimous things that every single woman who responded to my survey put on her top-twenty list. It is also the topic of many conversations at gyms, salons and brunches all over the globe.

Done at the right moment in a relationship, this is one of the most important and romantic things a man can do for his woman. This is one of those stories that you will tell your grandchildren later, if you're lucky. You can't skimp on this – this is major!

Ideally, a woman would love a proposal after six months to a year of dating someone exclusively. Unless he's very young, a man should definitely know by six months that this is a woman he wants to have as a wife or life-partner, or not. And I definitely mean a grown man, very close to or over 30 years of age, who's been in a monogamous and committed relationship with a woman he's seriously into.

Do not wait until she asks you why you haven't asked her yet, or where you expect this relationship to go. I've seen it happen so many times; the guy proposes only after getting an ultimatum – basically a 'step up or step off' deal. Or an unplanned pregnancy occurs and though the man is not ecstatic about his relationship, he feels the responsibility to 'do the right thing.' Those are both the wrong way to start a marriage and it can really take the magic out of things depending on how things turn out. In many cases it's the beginning of the end. I've also seen women just leave after three or more years of waiting for the guy to ask. That's so sad because that's a lot of time and emotion to give someone. Many men actually let 'the one' slip by them because for whatever reason they don't get their timing right, and they end up angry, hurt and jaded on love.

A man who loves his woman needs to act and just ask her! If you're over or around 30, and you're in love, you're more than ready for a long-term commitment with your beautiful woman. If you don't feel like you are, then maybe you should re-evaluate your relationship. But if you feel all the good feelings for your woman, don't waste precious time hemming and hawing. Pop the question! Make it special for her. It's something she'll never forget, so it has to be good. Whether you keep it simple or extravagant, make it heartfelt and romantic. Propose!

INVEST IN YOUR FUTURE!

94. Take her house hunting

This is a big one! So, you've decided to live together or you're both sure that this relationship is where you want to be for a long, long time. Your woman would love to hear you ask her if she'd like to go look at houses or condos– whatever dwelling you're interested in. To a woman it's exciting on two levels. First and obviously, she gets to go shopping, and for a house no less! But more importantly, she hears her man stepping up and going to the next level with her before she suggests it. That's huge! That's music to her ears! For both of you it is also a significant step toward financial freedom and a great life together. Investing in a home for the two of you is significant on so many levels. Remember to make sure you're realistic about what you can afford, and just go for it! Start comfortable and keep growing.

GROWING UP IS A GOOD THING!

95. *Be family-oriented*

A man who thinks like a family man is extremely attractive and valuable to a woman. A man who thinks about his family is responsible, considerate, attentive, and so many other positive characteristics that make a woman happy to be in his life. A family-oriented man makes sure his family or his future family will be taken care of. He plans ahead and is fully in it, enjoying the moments with the people he loves, and has his priorities clearly in order. It's not all you think about, but you start living your life and making big decisions with family in mind. When you really start thinking of other people like this, it's a great sign of growth and maturity. That's the kind of good, solid man every decent woman wants and appreciates.

Her Very Special Day...

96. Give her Her dream wedding

This is another huge one!! The wedding day is something that women look forward to since about the age of 3 or 4. No matter how modern and liberated we get, most of us still look forward to that day when we put on a beautiful dress and take vows with the man of our dreams. Most women don't plan on going through it more than once so we want it to be one of the great milestones that we'll remember forever. It's a magical moment in our lives and it should be as perfect as possible.

When you decide to take that step with your woman, do your absolute best to make this day special for her. Yes, we know that what really matters is the relationship and the life that comes after the wedding. But we still want the wedding day to be amazing.

By 'dream wedding' I don't mean it's got to be the most lavish or expensive wedding, but it should coincide with her vision. You should ask her what she'd ideally like to do that day and come up with a plan to get it done. This is her day to be a queen and she deserves the royal treatment.

Brides often complain that they are stressed when planning their weddings because the fiancé is hardly involved at all and she feels overwhelmed by all the details. In addition, the family on either side might impose their wishes and end up planning the wedding to their standards rather than the couple's. Ask her what she wants and make sure you keep your hand in the situation enough that it actually turns out the way she dreamed. Once you know what she wants, consider hiring a wedding planner to help with all the details. And if you are including your respective families in the planning, make it clear to them what level of input you want them to have so they don't step all over you.

Whether it's a simple or elaborate ceremony or even a weekend elopement, please your woman with her dream wedding and your married life will be off to a very happy start.

WOMEN LOVE A MANLY MAN!!

97. Be strong and masculine

Since the beginning of time straight on through the present, it seems women have always and will always love and be sexually attracted to strong and masculine men. Yes, we go for looks too and we enjoy both your physical and mental prowess. We love that you exude that uniquely male energy. When you get excited during sports, or pull us tightly into an embrace, or turn us inside out with a passionate kiss, it's a maddening turn on. So keep it up! We don't want a caveman, but we definitely don't want an effeminate mush who can't catch a football with his manicured nails or who can't walk the dog if it's bigger than a Yorkie.

A smart and grounded manly man knows who he is and can be strong without mistreating, verbally abusing, embarrassing or manhandling his woman. As a matter of fact, a strong and masculine man let's his woman shine as often as possible without feeling upstaged or less than. He wants her to be the princess in the relationship. It takes time to grow to that level of confidence and true masculinity. You have to strike that balance. That's when you'll really be hot, grown and sexy!

Crucially Important to Your Happiness

98. Learn the power of Yes!

This is another big one! There's a huge difference between being a 'Yes' man and saying 'Yes' to your woman. The one thing that the happily married couples I spoke with all have in common is that the men know how and when to say 'Yes.' They have figured out that their gonad size and function is not connected to being nice to their women. However, their sexual happiness and peaceful home life is directly connected! It appears to be a fact that men who say 'Yes' more often generally have much happier women in their lives, who in turn keep them very well fed and satisfied in any number of ways.

Remember, as the man in the relationship you're taking the lead with your example. Just because you're in a position of power and you 'wear the pants' doesn't mean you use your power to win fights, boss her around and dictate your way through life. As a smart and effective leader in your relationship, you must know the importance of agreeing as often as possible and keeping a peaceful and loving vibe in place. You'll catch many more bees with honey, so to speak, or in this case, you'll keep catching your honey's heart by being nicer and saying 'Yes' to her more often.

This is the Smart Man's Guide after all, and I'm sure you understand the importance and the outcome of handling your woman in a manner that pleases you both. It helps you build and maintain a solid and fun relationship. There's no need to constantly butt heads. Just say 'Yes!'

REMEMBER WAY BACK WHEN...?

99. Keep track of all the important dates

This is another area where woman and men can differ greatly, and it can be a crucial area where your happiness is concerned. This is your life partner if all goes well. Part of making things go well is planning, remembering, working at it. One of the most disappointing things women talk about is that their significant other forgot or didn't make a big deal about an important date, like a birthday or an anniversary.

Creating memories is a bi-product of how we live our lives. We want our memories to be great ones. That's how you build that great foundation that will carry you through the tough times and keep you living long and strong. Dates and details are really important to women and when men remember them it's very impressive. You don't have to keep it all in your head though. You can use a calendar. Put all the important dates in your blackberry, your home pc, office outlook, wherever you'll be reminded. It's not cheating, it's smart planning.

You are the special man in her life, so remind her how important she is to you by remembering the big dates – her birthday, your anniversary, or your month-iversary if you are newly dating. Try to remember the details of your first date, your first kiss, your first dance, etc.... Remember the times that marked some special moment in your relationship or in her life.

If you take her seriously by remembering details, she will take you and your relationship more seriously and you'll keep her happy. You make her day every time you remember an important date. Again, you're leading by example, so she'll follow your lead and cherish you even more, knowing she's spending her time and building a life with a good man.

Curl Her Toes Every Time!!

100. Keep that mercury boiling!

You can have a great sex life without much else going on in your relationship, but that sexual fire won't burn bright for very long without all the other elements of a strong relationship. You can have a great friendship and partnership, with only a mediocre sizzle in the bedroom, but how long will that keep you happy? I don't like mediocre one bit!

In order to keep you both in tune and desiring one another, you have to do a combination of taking care of yourself and taking care of each other. You both have to keep yourselves looking good, and help each other stay happy and uplifted. Since the man is the pace setter in a relationship, you need to find a way to turn that hot button on for her continuously. She'll likely take the reins from you, and turn you right back on. Be the initiator of great conversations, trips, massages, dinners and all these other suggestions, and you'll be the recipient of lots of kisses, affection, lovemaking, and hopefully, a long-lasting and wonderful relationship.

You can't always have that peak energy and excitement, but you have more than enough ideas now to keep those embers of attraction and passion burning. Keep your momentum going and keep her on her toes with fun, laughter and romance. That's a great way to shape your life together. You're likely to end up with curled toes all around, and that's just plain old good for your soul!

Have An Amazing Life!!

101. Live life to the fullest!

Do this one for both of you. Everything in this book is meant to have a positive impact on your relationship with that special woman in your life. One of the side effects of doing so many positive things is that you will also grow as an individual, not just as a great partner for her. So in closing I'm saying, keep it all up and keep moving forward at full blast. We get one life, today, this moment. Live each day like it's your happiest moment. Love her passionately. Grow more intimate. Live like you're the luckiest man in the world. Because you are. Laugh together as often as possible. Savor every moment and be grateful for everything you've been blessed with. Thank your Higher Power everyday with sincere humility and happiness. Always do your best for yourself and for your partner. Your enthusiasm will get you through everything you do and you'll make so many wonderful memories. Your efforts will be worth it. Hopefully, at the end of your life you will be able to look back and see what an amazing journey you've had and what a happy, loving and beautiful woman you had to share it all with, with both of you enjoying all the moments along the way.

Final Thoughts

After reading all these big and small ways you can please a woman, I hope you have a better understanding of how we think, what we like, and what it takes to keep us smiling and happy. You've now crossed the precipice and stepped into understanding us better. I expect you to run with it.

Women are definitely different from men, but our special needs are pretty basic. We want to be loved, accepted, respected and romanced. Plus, we want great, hot sex on a regular basis! It takes honesty, communication, maturity, patience and creativity to keep it all going. Lots of money wouldn't hurt either, but money alone is not enough to keep a woman happy. Men and woman are here to enrich each other's lives. The more we understand and respect each other, the more we'll appreciate and enjoy our lives together, and our journeys will be that much more fulfilling.

Love is precious, life is short, and timing is everything. Make it all as special and amazing as possible, for as long as possible. Thank you for letting me share some of my thoughts with you. I wish you much love, happiness and togetherness always!

Muah! (Big Kiss)

NLB

Quick Reference Tables

THE BASICS

1. Be honest and sincere with her and with yourself
2. Be free and clear
3. Be authentically nice and genuinely kind
4. Make her and your relationship a high priority in your life
5. She's your equal doesn't mean she wants to be the man
6. Be successful and stable
7. Be clean and neat
8. Be independent
9. Start small and slow and grow from there
10. Never give up the hunt – chase her, pursue her, woo her
11. Express yourself
12. Compliment her
13. Be respectful and respectable
14. Be level-headed and calm
15. Be a perfect gentleman

16. Know her, accept her, love her

17. Be committed to her

18. Listen

19. Be positive

20. Be loyal

21. Give her your undivided attention

22. Date night: dinner and a movie

23. Open up to her

Thoughtful & Sweet

24. Have fun

25. Be adventurous

26. Call her a sweet nickname

27. Plan a party together

28. Take her dancing

29. Learn to dance

30. Buy her a good book

31. Buy her coffee and a magazine

32. Invite her to know your family and friends

33. Put your money where your mouth is
34. Be her best friend
35. Be thoughtful and attentive
36. Take her shopping
37. Be level-headed and calm
38. Be emotionally supportive
39. Accompany her to family functions
40. Be a forward-thinking man with a sense of tradition
41. Keep her in the loop
42. Play nice
43. Be spontaneous
44. Take her to a live show
45. Buy her some delicious chocolate
46. Through thick and thin
47. Let her win
48. Support her when she's down
49. Show her what she means to you
50. Pray together

Très Romantique!

51. Be Mr. Romantic

52. Buy her flowers

53. Leave her love notes

54. Take her on a lunch date

55. Kiss frequently and deeply

56. Bring her breakfast in bed

57. Plan a weekend getaway

58. Draw her a rose bath

59. Have a candle lit dinner for two

60. Sing her a song

61. Pretend to read her palm

62. Plan a surprise party for her

63. Whisper in her ear

64. Look deep into her eyes

65. Go for long walks hand in hand

66. Candles, Incense, Music

67. Slow dance

68. Hold her close at night

69. Take her out often

70. Buy her pretty, sparkly things

71. Be loving, gentle and affectionate

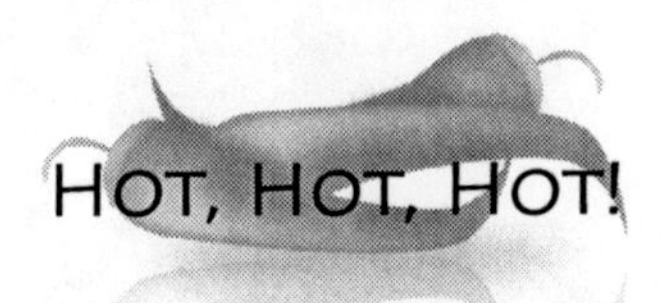

Hot, Hot, Hot!

72. Make her purr

73. Be driven and ambitious

74. Focus on her feet

75. Lick and suck all her erogenous zones

76. Buy her some sexy underwear

77. Take your time

78. Feast on her like she's the most delicious dessert

79. Love her like there's no tomorrow

80. Ladies first

The Total Package

81. Encourage her to follow her goals

82. Make her laugh, tap that A**

83. Sympathize when she's got cramps
84. Clean up
85. Be passionate
86. Be generous
87. Be patient
88. Be happy
89. Let her drive your car
90. Offer her your last bite
91. Celebrate accomplishments and create new traditions
92. Propose
93. Take her house hunting
94. Make a wish list for your future together
95. Be family-oriented
96. Give her Her dream wedding
97. Be strong and masculine
98. Learn the power of Yes
99. Keep track of all the important dates
100. Keep the mercury boiling
101. Live life to the fullest

About the Author

Lenaure Batista is a native New Yorker with Caribbean roots. She grew up surrounded by art and culture and her love of music, dance, writing, acting, film production and fitness have taken her to many interesting places and introduced her to people from all walks of life. You name it, she's probably done it, if it has to do with movement and creativity. She also enjoys traveling, participating in outdoor sports, supporting noble causes, spending time with her family and friends, and taking care of her adorable retriever pups.

LaVergne, TN USA
06 October 2009
160068LV00001B/16/P